THE SIXTH TANK BATTALION

CAPT. A/LT.-COL. R. A. WEST, V.C., D.S.O. AND BAR, M.C.
(Killed in Action, 2nd Sept. 1918.)
Commanded 6th Tank Batt., 23rd Aug. 1918 to 2nd Sept. 1918.

THE WAR HISTORY
OF
THE SIXTH
TANK BATTALION

PRIVATELY PRINTED

1919

All Rights Reserved.

FOREWORD

At Blangy-sur-Ternoise in April 1919 a meeting was summoned of all the officers, non-commissioned officers and men still serving with the battalion. At this meeting it was unanimously agreed to devote the private funds of the battalion to publishing the battalion history for the benefit of all surviving members and late members, and also of the next-of-kin of all who had fallen in battle or died since joining the battalion.

Since this history was written the cadre battalion has returned to England, and, contrary to our expectations and hopes, instead of forming the nucleus of a new Sixth Battalion, has been disbanded, those men who were retainable being drafted to and absorbed into new home battalions.

It is hoped that this book will serve not only to perpetuate the doings of the Sixth Tank Battalion, but to recall many friendships and happy and strenuous times shared by us all.

SOMERS.

Eastnor, Ledbury,
August 1919.

LIST OF ILLUSTRATIONS

	FACING PAGE
Capt. A/Lt.-Col. R. A. West, V.C., D.S.O., M.C.	*Frontispiece*
T/Lt.-Col. F. Summers, D.S.O., D.S.C.	97
Lt.-Col. C. M. Truman, D.S.O.	133
T/Major A/Lt.-Col. R. B. Wood	143
T/Lt.-Col. Lord Somers, D.S.O., M.C.	161
Sergt. Dudley, D.C.M.; Pte. Breakey, D.C.M.; Sergt. Prest, D.C.M.; Pte. Morrey, D.C.M.; Corporal Bussey, D.C.M.	205
Sergt. Brewer, D.C.M.; Pte. Quinn, D.C.M.; C.S.M. Cuthbert, D.C.M.; Pte. Siddell, D.C.M.; L.-Corporal Burden, D.C.M.	209
Medium Mark 'A' Tank; inset, C.S.M. Missen, D.C.M.	211

CONTENTS

CHAPTER I
EARLY DAYS, FORMATION, AND TRAINING AT BOVINGTON .   PAGE 1

CHAPTER II
EMBARKATION, AND FINAL TRAINING IN FRANCE . . 9

CHAPTER III
LIFE IN THE YPRES SALIENT, AND THIRD BATTLE OF YPRES   17

CHAPTER IV
REFITTING AND TRAINING BEFORE CAMBRAI . . . 44

CHAPTER V
CAMBRAI 52

CHAPTER VI
WINTER QUARTERS AND TRAINING 93

CHAPTER VII
SPRING OFFENSIVE 101

CHAPTER VIII

TRAINING FOR WHIPPETS 111

CHAPTER IX

AMIENS 117

CHAPTER X

FROM AYETTE TO THE HINDENBURG LINE . . . 141

CHAPTER XI

FROM TINCOURT TO ELINCOURT 165

APPENDICES

I. HONOURS AND AWARDS 205

II. ACTIONS 209

III. MEMBERS OF BATTALION 211

CHAPTER I

EARLY DAYS, FORMATION, AND TRAINING AT BOVINGTON

As a result of the Tank operations on the Somme, in the late summer and autumn of 1916, it was seen that Tanks would play an important part in the battles of the future, some persons even venturing to say that the new arm would be the means of ending the deadlock of trench warfare.

In October of 1916 it was decided to expand the four Experimental Companies in France into Battalions, and to form, in addition, five new Battalions in England.

On October 27, 1916, the whole of the estab- *At Thetford.*
lishment at Thetford moved to Wool in Dorsetshire. It must be explained that at Thetford there were two establishments, the Training Centre and the Area, the Centre being responsible for training in machine gunnery, 6-pounder, and all training other than Tank training. The "Area" carried on the work of Tank driving

in the secrecy which was such a notable feature of the early days of the Tanks.

On arriving at Wool the Centre formed the nucleus of No. 2 Battalion, under the command of Lieut.-Colonel R. J. Colsen, whilst the Area formed the nucleus of No. 3 Battalion. The Battalions at Bovington were numbered from 1 to 5, according to the positions they occupied in the camp.

Instructors' courses in gunnery, machine gun and revolver shooting were commenced in the first week of November. Whilst these were proceeding the new personnel began to arrive at the Battalion. The men who were transferred from the Training Centre were from the Motor Machine Gun Corps, and were formed into " A " Company under Captain F. S. Laskey. " B " and " C " Companies were formed almost entirely from men called up in groups under the Derby Scheme. During the last weeks of November the men arrived in great numbers, fresh from their civilian occupation. Each day large numbers were marched up from Wool Station, and passed before the Medical Officers, those who were passed fit being taken in hand by the Quartermasters' Department, and the rejected were sent back to their homes. It should be recorded that those men selected were very keen to get into the Tanks, and to take part in the most up-to-date method of fighting.

EARLY DAYS AT BOVINGTON

By the first week of December sufficient men had been selected to form the three Companies. "A" Company was placed under the command of Captain F. S. Laskey, "B" Company under Captain C. F. Hawkins, M.C., and "C" Company under Major Philip Hamond, D.S.O., M.C.

"A," "B," "C" Companies.

During the first weeks of December 1916, beyond the Instructors' courses, very little individual training was done, most of the time being spent on the square, getting the men to shape as soldiers before trying to turn them into Tank mechanics and gunners.

On December 13 a considerable number of the men and officers were sent to the Brigade for courses in the Vickers gun, Lewis gun, Hotchkiss gun, and 6-pounder. The remainder of the men and officers continued on the square at squad drill and physical training.

The Battalion was made up to strength with junior officers on December 12, when a considerable number of young officers arrived from the Machine Gun Corps Cadet Battalion at Bisley. These officers formed the bulk of the Tank commanders when the Battalion proceeded overseas.

From December 13 until February 24, 1917, individual training continued at high pressure.

No account of the early days of the Battalion can be considered complete without mention of the arrival of the Tanks at Bovington. The

Arrival of Tanks.

A.P.M. and his police, with numerous picquets of officers and men, guarded the road from Wool Station to the camp. All civilian traffic was stopped, and the inhabitants of the farms and cottages on the road were made to keep to the back rooms of their houses. On arrival at the camp the Tanks were parked in a compound in the woods below No. 1 Battalion's camp. This procedure was adopted each time Tanks were brought up by road. One farmer on being asked to keep to his back rooms replied he had no objection to helping the authorities to keep the "Secret of the Tanks," only unfortunately one had broken down, and had been towed into his farmyard, and there left for 48 hours.

"F" Battalion.
On December 29 the Battalion became known as "F" Battalion, and the Companies as 16, 17, and 18 Companies instead of "A," "B," "C."

Only a rest of two days at Christmas, then the work of individual training proceeded with increased vigour.

Change in Command.
On January 26, 1917, the command of the Battalion was taken over by Lieut.-Colonel F. Summers, D.S.O., D.S.C., *vice* Lieut.-Colonel R. J. Colsen. Colonel Summers had trained and led the original "D" Company on the Somme in the previous autumn.

The Companies were at this period placed under the command of the officers who were to proceed overseas with them. Major A. McC.

EARLY DAYS AT BOVINGTON

Inglis, D.S.O., who had seen considerable fighting with the Tanks on the Somme with the "Crème de Menthe," became O.C. 16 Company; Major C. F. Hawkins, M.C., commanding 17 Company, whilst Major Philip Hamond, D.S.O., M.C., continued with 18 Company.

By February 26 sufficient officers and men had completed their "individual training" to form a section in each Company. Numbers 1, 5, and 9 sections were formed and commenced straightway with the section training. From this time onwards intense rivalry was cultivated between sections. Each section had two huts for its quarters, which they re-decorated with distemper and limewash. The mess tables were scrubbed with bleaching soda, and the utensils polished until they shone like mirrors. The small plots at the end of the huts suddenly blossomed out into rockeries, the number of the section and mottoes proclaiming the merits of the sections being picked out in chalk and pieces of broken pottery. A Battalion Football League was started, and numerous games were played for the Championship. In a few weeks' time three more sections were added, and by May 6 the whole twelve sections had been completed, and had settled down to the work of training as sections.

Formation of Sections.

With Colonel Summers came a number of other officers who had fought with him in " D " Company on the Somme, and the Battalion

6 THE SIXTH TANK BATTALION

considered itself well favoured that it should have such a leavening of old Tank officers.

Intensive Training.
The Battalion commenced to mobilise on April 14, when a period of intensive training commenced. The men were hardened up by route marches and even more physical training. Section officers conducted compass and map reading expeditions. Refresher classes were run in each section for Lewis and 6-pounder. On the trench system around Gallows Hill, the section were taught the Tank tactics of the day; the training even included taping routes by night, and approach marches by day and by night.

The time was rapidly approaching when we should proceed overseas. It was a question greatly debated at the time as to whether we should obtain final leave. However, final leave was granted; one half of the Battalion going on Monday, April 21, returning Saturday, April 26, whilst the other half of the Battalion went Monday, April 28, and returned Saturday, May 3.

During the period of intensive training the Equipment Officers' Department had been busy, and by this time all the men had received the new equipment, designed for the Tank men, being infantry equipment with special revolver holster and ammunition pouches.

The finishing touches were put to the Battalion when each man had the now famous red and yellow cloth sewn on his shoulder-straps, and

EARLY DAYS AT BOVINGTON

the cloth Tank badge sewn on the right sleeve of his jacket.

About a week before leaving, Col. Summers offered a prize to the section which, on the sounding of the bugle, should be the first to march on to the parade ground in full marching order, complete in every detail. The *esprit de corps* was so keen that it was found necessary to announce that the bugle would sound between certain hours, as some of the sections had slept in full kit all the night, so as not to be caught unawares. The bugle was sounded about 3 P.M. on Sunday, May 12, and the prize was given to No. 12 section, under Captain W. Arnold. The same day the Battalion was inspected and addressed by Major-General F. Gore Anley, C.B., who in the course of his address made mention that " The whole eyes of the world would follow the achievements of the Tank Corps in the forthcoming operations, and he felt certain that 'F' Battalion would figure conspicuously in the rôle which the Tank Corps had to play to bring forth the Allies' greatest endeavour—that of Victory." *Inspection by Maj.-Gen. F. Gore Anley, C.B.*

On the morning of Monday, May 12, the Battalion paraded at Bovington for the last time. Every one was in full marching order. The Battalion was to move off to the port of embarkation in two trains, from Wool Station. The first detachment, led by Colonel Summers, was played down to the station by the Battalion *Move Overseas.*

band, and the band of the Middlesex Regiment. All Bovington turned out to see the first Battalion start for overseas. The second detachment, under Major Hamond, left some time later, and was played down by the band of the Middlesex Regiment, two journeys being considered too much for the Battalion band, which had only recently been formed, and pulled into shape by Captain A. R. Chapman. The trains arrived at Southampton Docks about 3 P.M. After detraining, and parading in Companies on the quay, the Battalion embarked, and made themselves as comfortable as circumstances would permit. It was on board the s.s. *Viper* that the souvenir habit first made its appearance; nearly all the men, and numbers of the officers, bought post-cards showing the s.s. *Viper* full steam ahead. At dusk the transport left the quay, and was soon off the Needles, where the transport picked up her escort of destroyers. The voyage across was perfectly eventless, and the *Viper* berthed alongside the quay at Le Havre at dawn. From this time onwards the Battalion was part of the Expeditionary Force.

CHAPTER II

EMBARKATION, AND FINAL TRAINING IN FRANCE

AT 7 A.M. the Battalion disembarked and formed up on the quay. Orders had been issued that a good show was to be put up, and the appearance of the Battalion, as they marched through the streets, was certainly very smart.

The band played us through the streets of the town, but the steep ascent of No. 1 Rest Camp, Senlac, soon caused them to stop. Indeed the march up hill in full kit tried nearly all.

At the Rest Camp we had our first experience under canvas. It was a tight fit, but still every one was keen, and in high spirits. The officers were accommodated in tents by the Officers' Rest House, and messed in the dining-room.

The date of departure for up the line was indefinite, so the time was filled in by a route march, in the direction of Coteville. The whole Battalion turned out for this event, the pack ponies being used to carry rations. After a drink of tea the men were allowed on the beach to bathe if they desired. This march passed into the Battalion legends, the distance covered increasing by leaps and bounds, until it is now gravely stated that we marched 35 to 40 kilometres in the d y.

The dining-cut habit, and the sense which directs soldiers to where good meals can be obtained, was cultivated from the earliest days, Tortoni's "The Moderne" being patronised by the officers as soon as permission to visit the town was given.

Departure from Le Havre.
The Battalion left Le Havre on Sunday, May 20, entraining at Pont 3 Gare des Voyageurs. The Railway Transport authorities evidently desired to give us a good impression of travelling in the British war zone, because the usual horse-boxes were missing, and all ranks were provided with respectable coaches. As this journey was the first of a long series of railway journeys in the war zone, it is worth recording that it was quickly found that the best way of getting boiling water for tea and coffee was to make friends with the engine driver, and obtain boiling water from the boiler.

Auchy-les-Hesdin.
The night was spent in the train at the new siding at Etaples. Next morning the train arrived at Auchy-les-Hesdin, where the Battalion detrained and fell in by Companies, and at once marched off to their billets in the village. Captain

FINAL TRAINING IN FRANCE

E. J. Hobbs, M.C., the Battalion Reconnaissance Officer, with an advance party, had arrived several days ahead, and guides were at hand to show the sections to their quarters. The billets for all ranks were generally good. This was the first time the inhabitants of Auchy had had a Tank Battalion billeted on them, and showed considerable pleasure in our stay there. In the hard times that were ahead the men frequently referred to the billets, and the good times they had had at Auchy-les-Hesdin.

We were here brigaded with " C " Battalion, and were in the 3rd Tank Brigade, commanded by Colonel Hardress Lloyd, D.S.O. *Under Command 3rd Tank Brigade.*

On arrival in France the section became more and more the unit. There were section billets, section messes, and section cook-houses. The rivalry between sections indeed became more intense.

On May 26, we, at full strength, were inspected by Brigadier-General H. J. Elles, D.S.O., commanding the Corps in France, in the grounds of the Château at Auchy. *Inspection by Brig.-Gen. H. J. Elles, D.S.O.*

The 1st of June saw the Battalion moved to the Corps Driving School at Wailly. The transportation was effected by motor omnibuses, the route being *via* St. Pol and Arras. The journey was of considerable interest to most of the Battalion, it being the first time they had seen a ruined city such as Arras. *Move to Wailly.*

12 THE SIXTH TANK BATTALION

Training at Wailly.

A certain number of Mark IV. Tanks were taken over, and driving instruction was organised over the old trench system between Wailly, Blairville, and Fischeux. The training here was extremely good, and the crews gained considerably in confidence. Owing to the limited number of Tanks the work was divided into three periods, the first starting at 4 A.M., and the last finishing at 8 P.M. Frequent demonstrations were given to Army and Corps commanders, illustrating the action of Tanks in assisting infantry in attacking a trench system. Generally, after these demonstrations, the Staff Officers would be given rides in the Tanks, good drops and jumps being carefully selected.

This period of training at Wailly was particularly valuable, because, besides the driving practice, officers and men became accustomed to making themselves comfortable under all circumstances.

The rigid rules on the question of dress were very considerably relaxed. Shirt sleeves, shorts, long stockings, and Highlanders' short puttees became the rule, everything of as light a colour as possible, during the extremely hot weather. A long staff, after the manner of an alpenstock, instead of the short crook, was another feature introduced.

The salvage work on the old British and German trench system had not been anything

FINAL TRAINING IN FRANCE 13

like completed. Many German dug-outs, of an enormous depth, had hardly been touched. In the spare time, parties from the Battalion explored these workings, and soon acquired the art of making life comfortable by means of unconsidered trifles.

On June 5, just previous to the Battle of Messines, two sections of the Tanks were ordered to proceed to Croiselles and move towards Henin-sur-Cojeul, and to show themselves in daylight, in such a manner that the German aircraft must see them, the object being to mislead the enemy into believing that an offensive would take place in that neighbourhood.

Towards the end of the training a point-to-point cross-country race was organised. Each section had a race over the course against time, and the crew and bus with the best time was selected to compete in the Company race. Finally on Sunday, June 9, the three Companies competed in the final. The result was that 16 Company was first, 2nd Lieut. V. G. Sanders; 18 Company second, 2nd Lieut. H. Pearson, D.C.M.; and 17 Company third, 2nd Lieut. W. D. Howell. It is doubtful if Mark IV.'s ever before or since have attained the speed they did that afternoon. Rumour said that all sorts of devices were resorted to in order to get the extra speed out of the buses.

On the occasion of one of these races one

keen Tank commander kept his bus in fourth until actually crossing the famous Sunken Road, intending to slip his secondary gears from 2 to 1 as he descended. His gearsmen got them out of 2 right enough, but were unable to get them into 1. The Tank rushed madly down the slope, half climbed the other bank, and then dropped back again, continuing in this way until it finally came to rest at the bottom.

After a fortnight of training at Wailly we returned to Auchy-les-Hesdin, where training continued.

Training at Merlimont. The next visit was to the Corps Gunnery School at Merlimont. Each Company was to go for a week, 16 Company leading off, 18 Company following at an interval of a week. Work started early in the morning, parties being detailed to shoot on the 6-pounder range, or the machine-gun range on the dunes. Bathing parties were arranged each day under an officer, and the whole Company would sometimes be in the water together.

Drawing of Tanks. The Battalion drew their first Fighting Tanks at Erin on June 16. The party drawing them proceeded to central workshops at Erin by lorry, and drew nineteen Tanks and trekked to Auchy with them. After 18 Company had gone to Merlimont it had been intended that 17 Company should follow, but it was found that time would not permit this, as the Battalion

FINAL TRAINING IN FRANCE 15

had to be equipped and ready to move to the "Forward Area" by the end of the month.

The week following was occupied in drawing Tanks from Erin, and trekking them, by road, to Auchy-les-Hesdin, where a Tankodrome had been made. Shortly the whole Battalion was equipped with Tanks, 12 Fighting Tanks and 2 Supply Tanks per Company. The organisation was that in each Company there were three Fighting Sections, each with four Tanks (two males and two females), and one Supply Section with two Supply Tanks. It was finally arranged that each Company should have one section entirely of females.

There was considerable amusement and excitement over the naming of the Tanks; of course all had to commence with the letter F. Some of these names afterwards became famous. *Naming of Tanks.*

Each section tried its utmost to turn its buses out as smart as possible. A complete overhaul was made. The inside was scoured and painted. All brass unions were polished, and the whole interior got up in a way that would not have disgraced the traditions of the Navy.

Several sections adopted Section signs, which were painted on the noses of the Tanks. The neatest idea was that which was later on adopted by 16 Company, Major Inglis's Company. The Company was represented by a hand of cards and each section had a suit allotted to it. Thus

F. 1 had the ace of hearts painted on each side of the nose. The other sections had spades, diamonds, and clubs, the section being indicated by the suit, and the number by the card. One of 17 Company's sections adopted the mailed fist and Dagger as its sign, whilst in No. 9 section each Tank crew commander dipped his hand in red paint, and pressed it against the nose of the bus, thus christening it with the sign of the blood-stained hand.

By the last week in June the whole Battalion was ready for action, on whatever part of the front the great ones should assign to us.

We were soon to feel the benefit of the careful training, individual, section, and Company, of the last six months, and to appreciate the careful and thorough organisation which had been lavished on the Battalion.

Every one was conscious of the excellent feeling and spirit of comradeship which existed between all ranks. But it was only later that all recognised to the full how the constant association of officers and men, working together, either on courses or in sections, had created an *esprit de corps* which was to pull the Battalion through the tough times to come.

CHAPTER III

LIFE IN THE YPRES SALIENT, AND THIRD BATTLE OF YPRES

IT is always a mystery how rumours originate. Although the secret of our destination was perfectly kept, yet about the end of June old hands were talking knowingly of the salient. There has only been one salient on the British Front, that rough angle of trench systems guarding the ruins of Ypres and its water-logged lands.

On July 2 the move was commenced by 16 Company trekking the Fighting Tanks to the railhead at Erin. The day following 16 Company entrained at Erin at 2 P.M., and left for Oosthoek Wood, under Major A. McC. Inglis, D.S.O., arriving there about 10.30 P.M., where they detrained and camouflaged. The same day 17 Company left Auchy for Erin, under Major C. F. Hawkins, D.S.O., M.C., and entrained for Oosthoek the following day, whilst 18 Company, under Major P. Hamond, D.S.O., M.C., left Auchy for Erin on July 4, and entrained for Oosthoek on the 5th, arriving about 11 P.M.

Move to "The Salient."

the same night. By 3 A.M. on the morning of July 6, the whole of the Fighting Tanks of the Battalion had arrived in the Wood, and were camouflaged in such a way that no enemy airmen would take the mounds and hummocks of green stuff for Tanks.

On the night of the 4th, 17 Company had their first experience of shell-fire, the enemy long-range guns worrying the Woods for several hours.

Oosthoek Wood.

It will be as well here to give some description of the Wood and surrounding country. Oosthoek Wood was just off Elverdinghe–Poperinghe Road, in a central position between Poperinghe, Elverdinghe, and Vlamertinghe. To those who know Flanders it is just one of those rather dense woods of young oak trees. There were the remains of breastworks which had evidently been constructed in 1915, when there was danger of the enemy breaking through. The works now were in a bad state of repair, but in the small dug-outs and shelters it was possible to accommodate the crews, and make things fairly comfortable.

First Casualties.

In his systematic manner the Bosche used to worry the camp with long-range guns. It was here that the first casualties to the Battalion occurred. On the night of the 4th a shell burst near the guard, supplied by 17 Company, killing one man, Private T. Atkinson, and wounding two others, Privates H. Atkinson and E. Bingham. "C" Battalion, on the north side of the railway,

LIFE IN THE YPRES SALIENT 19

had even worse luck. A shell landed in their headquarters, causing several casualties, and another landed in the cook-house.

As the enemy paid too much attention to the Wood, it was decided to shift the camp, which had been commenced, farther back, and to leave only a guard and necessary working-parties there.

On July 6 the whole Battalion, less the guard, moved to La Louvie, on the Poperinghe–Crombeck Road, where, in another wood, well concealed from inquisitive airmen, another camp was established. *Move to La Louvie.*

The supply sections, with Tanks, arrived at Oosthoek Wood on the night of the 6th, and later joined the Battalion in the new camp. In a short time Battalion life was going on again in full swing. Spare tarpaulins, thrown over saplings, lashed to two trees, made good messes both for officers and other ranks, and although the Wood resembled a gipsy encampment, yet it was surprising how comfortable one became under canvas in La Louvie Wood. *Supply Sections.*

It will be as well to describe the life at the camp at La Louvie and then that of the detachment at Oosthoek.

At La Louvie it was impossible to have tents arranged in orderly rows as is the custom with military camps. All that could be done was to keep each company's tentage grouped together, and to have the cook-houses at the end of the camp. There would be an early morning parade *Life at La Louvie, Oosthoek.*

and inspection unless conditions made it impossible. Breakfasts at 8 A.M. under mess bivouacs. Owing to the impossibility of obtaining enough room to have Company messes, the section and Company headquarters' messes continued in the *al fresco* style. 16 Company had five shanties, presided over by the Major and his four section commanders. 17 Company and 18 Company each had a headquarters' mess and a large shed with a corner detailed to each of the sections. The Battalion headquarters had a Nissen Hut, which also did service as Colonel Summers' office.

The band at this time flourished exceedingly, playing its selections each evening, the R.S.M., A. Macer, acting as a whip to the band, and generally fathering it in its infant days.

A benevolent G.H.Q. seemed to have arranged a splendid system of lorries both ways along the Crombeck Road to and from Poperinghe. The majority of the Battalion took full advantage of this fact to lorry hop into the town. Owing to the great concentration of troops in Flanders for the famous Passchendaele Push, Poperinghe was always surging with troops. All regiments and arms of the British Army were to be met there.

It came to one's turn to go up to Oosthoek, and act as guard and maintenance party at the Tankodrome. The shelling was not severe by any means, but it was advisable to sleep in the shelters left in the old breastwork. Rations

LIFE IN THE YPRES SALIENT

and mails would come up every day. Those not actually detailed for guard had plenty of work to do fitting the new unditching gear, which came into use just before the Battle of Ypres. Great care had to be taken to avoid being seen from a Bosche observation balloon. Then there were thousands of rounds of ammunition to be filled into Lewis pans. Lewis guns had to be cleaned and oiled periodically, likewise the 6-pounders. Also the engines had to be started and cleaned frequently.

No more casualties were caused, however, by enemy long-range shelling, although he continued to annoy the Wood. No one who was there is likely to forget the night the enemy " set up " three truck loads of 12" shells. The R.G.A. had a 12" howitzer just off the railway, through the Wood, about 200 yards from the Tankodrome. The Bosche had been busy with counter-battery work for some time, and that particular night the gunners were changing position. The howitzer had already left, and the ammunition, loaded into trucks, awaited an engine. A lucky shot from a long-range gun struck a truck, and set fire to the charges; soon the truck was burning merrily. The gunners fled through the Tank park in search of cover. The sentry and guard sought shelter beneath the buses, and waited for the worst. There was a terrific explosion with a mighty rush of air, a pause, and then a deluge of metal. Luckily no damage was done. Some one crept out to see how matters stood, and then it was seen that there were another two to go, so another dive underneath, and another anxious wait, until the deluge of metal had ceased. Not a single man or Tank was hurt, although the traffic man at " Dirty Bucket Corner," a quarter of a mile away, had his arm smashed.

Whilst at Auchy, the Adjutant, Captain W. H. Mortimore, left the Battalion on account of ill-health, Captain E. J. Hobbs, M.C., temporarily became Adjutant to the Battalion, and Captain C. P. Voss, M.C., became Battalion Reconnaissance Officer. Under Captain Voss, and the Company Reconnaissance Officers, the reconnaissance work proceeded. First of all the route was chosen from the Wood to the Canal, then from the Canal to the jumping-off point at Weiltje. The approach march had to be done in three stages, so " lying up " places had also to be chosen. After a thorough reconnaissance of the ground behind our front line, the next thing was to gain some knowledge of the various objectives. The R.O.'s, by means of vertical and oblique aeroplane photos, pointed out and drilled into the crew commanders and N.C.O.'s the places they would have to clear up on the day they would go over the top. After this journeys were made to the front line, and advan-

Reconnaissance Work.

LIFE IN THE YPRES SALIENT 23

tageous points, where peeps over the parapet were taken at such places as Bosart Farm, Pommern Redoubt, Somme Farm, and Kansas Cross.

During this time the tracks and roads in the salient lived up to their evil reputation, and there were many experiences during these reconnaissance trips.

By the end of the month all that could be done to make officers and men familiar with the places they had to take had been done. Then came the job of preparing forward dumps of petrol, oil, and grease, to replenish the Tanks on the journeys to the " jumping-off " point and after action. The final dump was prepared at St. Jean by Major Philip Hamond, D.S.O., M.C., and C.S.M. J. O'Keefe, M.M., with a working-party with Ford box-bodies.

On the night of July 25, 17 Company left the Tankodrome at 9.30 P.M., and reached Trois Tours at 3.30 A.M. A guard was left on the Tanks, and after camouflaging, the remainder of the personnel returned to camp. *Approach Marches.*

Whilst awaiting the arrival of the Tanks at Trois Tours, Captain W. Mann, second in command of 17 Company, and 2nd Lieut. J. C. Porter were killed by a shell hitting the dug-out in which they were sheltering.

On the 26th orders were received postponing zero 72 hours. Advantage was taken of this delay to give additional rest to the crews.

On the evening of the 27th the crews of 17 Company left La Louvie by lorry, and arrived at Trois Tours, taking over their Tanks from the guard. The Company started from Trois Tours at 9.30 P.M. and trekked to Murat Farm, arriving at 11.30 P.M., where they again camouflaged, and left the Tanks under a guard.

The next night both 16 and 17 Companies' crews went up in lorries, 16 Company to Oosthoek Wood and 17 Company to Murat Farm.

The start from Oosthoek Wood was made by 16 Company at 9.30 P.M.; the approach march was made over the same route as that chosen by 17 Company three nights earlier. The march was without incident, and Murat Farm was reached by 2.30 A.M. In the meantime 17 Company left Murat Farm and crossed the Yser Canal by Essex Farm, *via* Frascati. During this approach several casualties occurred. Captain L. C. Bond, M.C., Lieut. A. S. W. Willis, 2nd Lieut. R. P. Foster, Lance-Corporal A. J. Frost, and Gunner A. J. Lloyd (Workshop Company), attached to 17 Company, were wounded.

No. 16 Company arrived at St. Jean at 2.30 A.M. July 30. Both Companies fitted their Tanks with spuds at St. Jean.

On the night of the 30th the route from St. Jean to the starting-point—Oxford Road, and from Oxford Road to the British front line—was taped out.

THIRD BATTLE OF YPRES

At 3.50 A.M. zero, on the morning of July 31, 17 Company left Oxford Road under Major C. F. Hawkins, M.C., and proceeded into battle, whilst 16 Company, under Major A. McC. Inglis, D.S.O., left St. Jean and proceeded into battle at 9.30 A.M. 18 Company, under Major Philip Hamond, D.S.O., M.C., proceeded as far as Reigersburg, and there awaited further orders.

The action as regards this Battalion is divided into two parts: *Plan of Battle.*

(1) The attack on the Black Line.
(2) The attack on the Green Line.

No. 17 Company was ordered to attack the Black Line with three sections of four Tanks, advancing with the infantry of the 165th and 166th Brigades, from the Blue Line at zero plus 1 hour 15 minutes.

No. 16 Company was ordered to attack the Green Line, with two sections of four Tanks, to advance with the infantry of the 164th Brigade, from the Black to the Green dotted line at zero plus 6 hours 20 minutes, followed up by the "Mopping-up Section," of four Tanks.

No. 18 Company remained in Corps Reserve during this action.

BLACK LINE

The twelve Tanks of No. 17 Company crossed Oxford Road at zero, F. 36, F. 38, and F. 39 being led by their officers. F. 23 and F. 21 in the centre, and F. 28 on the right, reached their objective, the Black Line. All *Actions of Individual Tanks.*

except F. 36 and F. 38 were very late, owing to the difficulty encountered in advancing over the bad ground.

F. 36. "Furious."

On the left, whilst advancing to her objective, captured two Germans by the side of a field gun, also knocked out a machine gun in Border House. She then became ditched, and as the unditching gear had already been shot away, could not be got out. The officer in charge was wounded.

F. 38. "Firefly."

Reached her objective, and was then sent for by the infantry. Knocked out a machine gun 150 yards south-west of Spree Farm. After patrolling the Black Line again, while searching for machine guns, this Tank received a direct hit, which stopped her. Afterwards she received three more direct hits, and was burnt out. The officer in charge was killed.

F. 39. "Formosa."

Dispersed snipers and knocked out a machine gun in Capricorn Trench, and cleared out twenty of the enemy in the communication trench leading to the Capricorn Keep, who were holding up the infantry. She then returned to the rallying-point.

F. 23. "Foggie."

Arrived late and proceeded to Bank Farm, where the infantry were signalling for assistance. The enemy were cleared out, and returned towards Pommern Redoubt. Owing to a leaking radiator, this Tank became stopped at Plum Farm.

F. 21. "Five Knights."

Proceeded to Plum Farm, where the infantry were held up by four machine guns. The guns were silenced and the crew of one captured. She went on then to

THIRD BATTLE OF YPRES

Pommern Redoubt, and drove out the garrison. After patrolling in front, whilst the infantry were consolidating, she returned home.

F. 28. "*Formidable.*"

Having been ditched on the way up, was fetched by the infantry to Pommern Redoubt. Fire was opened out in the direction pointed out by the infantry. Six of the crew were wounded by machine-gun bullets. While manœuvring to bring the port guns to bear, she became ditched. The guns were taken out of the Tank and used from a shell-hole; later in the day the Tank was unditched and returned home.

F. 27. "*Fighting Mac.*"
F. 37. "*Ferocious.*"
F. 22. "*Flying Fox.*"

Reached approximately the Blue Line; the two former were stopped by mechanical trouble.

F. 30. "*Flaming Fire.*"

Before reaching the Blue Line, received a direct hit and was burnt out.

F. 26. "*Fearless.*"
F. 25. "*Fums Up.*"

The former was ditched, and the latter broke the Coventry chain, both before reaching the Blue Line.

Green Line

At zero the two sections forming the first wave left the point of assembly at St. Jean for their position of deployment on the Black Line. At 4.20 A.M. the four "mopping up" Tanks, which formed the second wave, left the point of assembly, followed by two Supply Tanks and a Wireless Tank. This Company had great difficulty between the German front line and the Blue

Line, owing to the bad going. In spite of frequent uses of the unditching gear, several Tanks became hopelessly ditched.

F. 13. "*Falcon.*"

In crossing the German front line became ditched three times, but proceeded, and fire was opened south of Spree Farm on the Germans, who were still holding up the infantry in this place. On the infantry commencing to advance from the Black Line, with this Tank leading, she received a direct hit, which killed the officer in charge and completely wrecked the Tank.

F. 15. "*Fifinella.*"

This Tank became ditched twice in the German frontline system; the last time, although every effort was made under heavy fire for four hours, she could not be moved. During this time the officer in charge and a member of the crew were wounded.

F. 11. "*Fizyama.*"

Had given a good deal of mechanical trouble before action, and though repaired, broke down after starting, and never reached the British front line.

F. 12. "*Friar Tuck.*"

Started late owing to mechanical trouble, but caught up the other Tanks; she was ditched twice in the German front-line system, and the last time could not be got out.

F. 9. "*Feu Follet.*"

This Tank was ditched in the German front-line system, and owing to the unditching gear having been shot away, had to be dug out, thus causing a big delay. After unditching the Tank proceeded to the Green Line and was in action. As the infantry were consolidating, and did not require help, the Tank returned to the Company rallying-point near Hill 35. Whilst here

THIRD BATTLE OF YPRES 29

the petrol tank was hit by a fragment of shell, and the Tank put out of action.

F. 6. " Feu D'Artifice."

This Tank became ditched in the German front line, and the engine overheating, was unable to be got out.

F. 7. " Feu de Ciel."

This Tank was ditched four times crossing the German front-line system, and the last time could not be got out.

F. 5. " Firefly."

Became ditched in the German front-line system, and owing to the strain thereby imposed, mechanical trouble supervened. The crew of this Tank were transferred to F. 1.

F. 1. " Firespite."

In crossing the German front-line system, this Tank became ditched and five of the crew wounded. A new crew from F. 5 was obtained. The Tank got out and proceeded into action on the Green Line. Finding the infantry were consolidating, she returned home, but became ditched in crossing the German front-line system. As the unditching gear had been shot away, the Tank could not then be got out.

F. 3. " Frolic."

This Tank was ditched four times whilst crossing the German front-line system, and finally put out of action by a fragment of shell striking the magneto. The officer in charge of the Tank was wounded.

F. 4. " Flint."

This Tank proceeded to the Green Line, but arriving late, found the infantry already in possession, and not requiring help. On the return journey the Tank became very badly ditched, near Polizee Wood. As

30 THE SIXTH TANK BATTALION

the unditching gear had been shot away, the Tank could not then be got out.

F. 10. "*Feu D'Enfer.*"

This Tank was one of the "mopping-up" Tanks; nothing is known of her journey to the Black Line. She came into action after F. 13 had been knocked out. After getting into action she became ditched, but got out and proceeded to the Green Line. Owing to the shortage of petrol, she returned to the Company rallying-point, where she received a direct hit, killing the officer and severely wounding the majority of the crew.

F. 16. *Wireless Tank.*

This was the signal Tank, and proceeded to its station near Weiltje Dug-Out, but the wireless apparatus having broken down, she returned later in the day.

F. 17. "*Follow the Crowd.*"

Supply Tank. This Tank became ditched three times in the German front-line system, and owing to the delay thus caused, after unditching for the last time, was too late to be of any assistance, and returned home.

F. 19. "*Fill Up.*"

Supply Tank. Same as above.

Casualties. The following officers and other ranks were killed in action July 31, 1917 :

2nd Lieut. N. H. A. Ready	. .	. 16	Company.
,, B. Seymour	. .	. ,,	,,
,, E. Coleman	. .	. 17	,,
2145 Gunner Allen, A. P.	. .	. 16	,,
92562 ,, Drury, G.	. .	. ,,	,,
62549 Corporal Baldock, J.	. .	. ,,	,,
92589 Gunner Wells, C. D.	. .	. ,,	,,
69254 ,, Brown, A.	. .	. ,,	,,
69472 ,, Lewis, N.	. .	. 17	,,

THIRD BATTLE OF YPRES 31

92457 Gunner Ashplant, W. . . 16 Company.
2691 Lance-Corporal Parkinson, A. . ,, ,,

The following officers and other ranks were wounded in action July 31, 1917 :

2nd Lieut. R. G. Wheatley .		.	16 Company.	
,,	E. S. Lennard .	.	,,	,,
,,	N. T. O'Connell .	.	,,	,,
,,	A. E. Smith	.	,,	,,
,,	A. W. Fletcher .	.	17	,,
38512 Gunner Entwhistle, J. A.		.	16	,,
38497 ,,	Ross, S. J. .	.	,,	,,
92483 ,,	Pettifer, W. J.	.	,,	,,
92565 Sergeant Hornsey, C. G.		.	,,	,,
762 Corporal Newey, L. .		.	,,	,,
38884 Lance-Corporal Pick, G.		.	17	,,
95512 Sergeant Harrington, G. W.		.	,,	,,
69368 Gunner Hayes, W. .		.	,,	,,
38943 Sergeant Passmore, F. A.		.	,,	,,
69294 Gunner Marshall, J. W.		.	,,	,,
38492 ,,	M'Lellan, W.	.	16	,,
69536 ,,	Dudley, S. R.	.	,,	,,
38537 ,,	Lee, W. H. .	.	,,	,,
38736 ,,	Hewson, A. W.	.	17	,,
92776 ,,	Green, F.	.	,,	,,
38644 ,,	Dunstan, G. .	.	,,	,,
38407 ,,	Swarbrick, J. S.	.	16	,,
92600 ,,	Walsh, W. T.	.	,,	,,
92523 ,,	Muirhead, J. .	.	,,	,,
92549 ,,	Garvie, D. .	.	,,	,,
69421 ,,	Holden, W. L.	.	,,	,,
92636 ,,	Tucker, A. .	.	17	,,
69362 ,,	Herbert, S. .	.	,,	,,
38725 ,,	Reeve, C. V. .	.	,,	,,
92621 ,,	Gill, H.	.	,,	,,
31451 Sergeant Davidson, F. R.		.	18	,,
69284 Gunner Bowers, W. .		.	,,	,,
38514 ,,	Flint, P. A. .	.	,,	,,
38829 ,,	Dolphin, A. .	.	17	,,

38932	Gunner	Wilson, R.			17 Company.
92771	„	Croucher, G.			„
69632	„	Newberry, E.		„	„
69640	„	Peck, G.		Brigade Signal Section.	
69721	„	Taylor, S. W.	„	„	„

The following Honours and Awards were granted :

Military Cross.

2nd Lieut. A. E. Renwick.
  „   C. H. J. Tolley.
  „   A. W. Fletcher.

Military Medal.

95512 Sergeant Harrington, G. W.
38746 Gunner Dowse, G.
92352   „   Corby, J.
38894   „   Franckombe, C.
92637   „   Young, B. S.
 2256   „   Tarry, A. J. W.
92565 Corporal Hornsey, C. G.

Distinguished Conduct Medal.

69715 Corporal Cuthbert, F. W.

Salvage Work. The next day or so after the action was occupied in trying to salve as many of the Tanks as possible. In some cases, after two or three nights' work, a Tank would be so damaged by shell-fire, that it had to be handed over to salvage. The weather conditions made the work of salvage exceedingly difficult, as it rained continually for a week, commencing on July 31. On August 6, however, the weather changed, and the ground commenced to dry up somewhat.

On August 7 all available Tanks were brought

THIRD BATTLE OF YPRES 33

back to Oosthoek Wood. Salvage operations continued during the ensuing week, under great difficulties. For the next ten days life proceeded normally. The weather continued to clear up, and several route marches were made.

On the 18th orders were received for 18 Company to co-operate with the 61st Division. It was eventually decided that only two sections were to go into battle, Numbers 9 and 10. On the night of August 20, eight Tanks moved up from Reigersburg to St. Jean, and camouflaged there. On the night of the 21st the crews of the two sections left La Louvie, being given a great send-off by 16 and 17 Companies. The approach march started at about 9 P.M. *via* Weiltje and the Gravenstafel Road to the front line at Spree Farm. The approach march was of extraordinary difficulty, the nature of the ground being such that the only possible way was to go in single file along the road, which had been shelled, and in many places blown up by mines, for had one Tank gone off the track it would have been utterly unable for those behind to pass.

Preparations for Attack on Aug. 22.

Operations.

1. On Z day the 61st Division (left Division, XIX. Corps) will establish itself on the Green Line.

Two sections of No. 18 Company will co-operate with the 61st Division. The attack by the 61st Division will be carried out by the 164th Brigade, plus one Battalion of the 183rd Brigade. The remainder of the

Plan of Attack.

D

183rd Brigade, and the 182nd Infantry Brigade, will be in Divisional Reserve.

The 15th Division will attack on the right with two sections of Tanks from " C " Battalion, and the 48th Division, XVIII. Corps, on the left, with the Tanks from " D " Battalion.

Tanks.

    2. No. 18 Company will be in the following position by zero :

    No. 9 Section on the Weiltje–Gravenstafel Road 500 yards to the left of Spree Farm.

    No. 10 Section, 300 yards behind No. 9 Section.

The Attack.

    3. At zero the infantry will advance and capture the enemy system up to and including the Green Line.

    No. 9 Section will co-operate in the attack.

    No. 10 Section will act as a second wave—one Tank being detailed to each of the routes of No. 9 Section.

    No. 1 route will be taken by F. 42 with F. 46 in support.

    No. 2 ,, ,, ,, F. 45 ,, F. 47 in support.

    No. 3 ,, ,, ,, F. 43 ,, F. 48 in support.

    No. 4 ,, ,, ,, F. 41 ,, F. 49 in support.

The second wave of Tanks (No. 19 Section) will work in couples, thus :

F. 46 and F. 47 must be prepared to replace F. 42 or F. 45, and F. 48 and F. 49 to replace F. 43 or F. 41 on receiving the signal " Am broken down."

If F. 42 is broken down F. 46 will replace him, but if F. 46 is also broken down F. 47 will replace F. 42.

Barrage.

    4. The barrage will be put down approximately on a line 200 yards in front of the present front line. The first lift will be at zero, plus five minutes, and the rate of advance 100 yards in five minutes until zero plus ten

THIRD BATTLE OF YPRES

minutes, and subsequently at the rate of 100 yards in eight minutes.

Consolidation.

5. The protective barrage will be formed from 500 to 300 yards in front of the Green Line.

All Tanks on reaching the line will cover the work of consolidation by patrolling in front, under cover of the protective barrage.

Each Tank will remain for thirty minutes after the infantry arrive at their objective, in the sector of the objective included in the Tank's route, and will then return to the rallying-points at St. Jean, unless they are engaged fighting, or there are any requests outstanding for their assistance. If the advance is held up, Tank commanders will render all assistance to the infantry, and will not return until the line is consolidated. In the event of a counter-attack, Tanks will remain to assist the infantry. The S.O.S. signal will be a succession of green Véry lights.

Synchronising Watches.

6. Each section will send an officer to Company headquarters at 2 A.M. on YZ night to take Brigade time.

Report Centre.

7. From 9 P.M. YZ night, Company headquarters will be at Weiltje Dug-outs, which will also be Battalion Report Centre from zero.

Preliminary Instructions.

8. Preliminary No. 2 issued July 17, where not at variance with these Orders, are to be read as supplemental to these Orders.

9. The attacking Tanks will have the following objectives :

36 THE SIXTH TANK BATTALION

1st. Pond Farm, Hinder Gott, Schuler Gallery, Schuler Farm.
2nd. Along Gravenstafel Road to Schuler Gallery.
3rd. Dug-outs at a point central between Schuler Farm and Pond Farm; a point central between Somme Farm and Kansas Cross. Kansas House-Cross Cottages to the north of Somme Farm.
4th. Somme, Gallipoli, Martha House to the right of Kansas Cross.

F. 41. "*Fray Bentos.*"

Action of Tanks on Aug. 22.

Proceeded from point of development five minutes before zero. At zero the enemy put down a heavy barrage, which was successfully passed through. Tank received two hits by fragments, which passed through right outer track adjuster. Whilst approaching Somme Farm came under heavy machine-gun fire, and opened fire with left 6-pounder in that direction, and silenced it. At 5.30 A.M. Tank F. 43 was seen on the right, also a "C" Battalion Tank was seen on the right. At 5.45 A.M. came under heavy machine-gun fire from Gallipoli, and whilst engaging this target the Tank crew commander was wounded in the neck by a fragment of a bullet. Whilst the section commander was taking the crew commander's place the Tank became ditched. Two separate attempts were made to put on the unditching gear, under heavy fire, and one of the crew was killed whilst outside the Tank. The machine guns, firing from Gallipoli, were engaged by 6-pounder and silenced. Our infantry at this time, about 7 o'clock, went back, leaving the Tank isolated. The enemy followed up closely, but were engaged by the one 6-pounder which could be brought to bear, and the Lewis guns and a rifle, which were taken into the Tank. The N.C.O. got out of the Tank and made his way to the British lines to prevent our infantry shooting any

THIRD BATTLE OF YPRES

one coming out of the Tank, as the Tank was being sniped at by both our infantry and the enemy. Later on our infantry were stopped by displaying a white rag from the porthole of the Tank. After remaining in the Tank until 9 P.M. on the 24th inst., it was left by the officers and the crew, all of whom were, by this time, wounded. A covering party for the Tank was arranged for, with the infantry and the Lewis guns placed at their disposal. During the time the Tank was out, viz. 22nd, 23rd, and 24th, the enemy, in small parties, made several attempts to get in the Tank by bombing, and were successfully beaten off with machine-gun, rifle, and revolver fire.

F. 42. " *Faun.*"

Received a direct hit whilst lined up at the starting-point, before zero, putting one turret out of action, on right side, and wounding one man. Proceeded at zero for about 200 yards, under heavy fire, and then became ditched. The officer and all the crew became casualties while putting on the unditching gear. An officer and a fresh crew were sent up, as soon as the officer commanding the Company was informed of the situation, but the Tank could not be unditched, owing to heavy fire. The Tank was got back on the night of the 23.8.17, and brought to the Company rallying-point.

F. 43. " *Fritz Phlattner.*"

Proceeded into action behind F. 41, and then went to the left of Somme Farm, and came into action there. Under heavy machine-gun fire all the time. Then became ditched beyond Somme, after putting on unditching gear chain broke, and officer ordered the crew to dig her out. Owing to the heavy fire one of the crew was wounded. The officer ordered all of the crew out with the guns. He was then shot himself. The sergeant ordered the crew to retire with the guns, and remained with the officer in a shell-hole till he died. The sergeant and two men were wounded, the former severely, whilst with his officer.

F. 45. "Fiducia."

Proceeded at zero in front of the infantry, and came into action immediately on crossing our front line. Shortly afterwards became ditched near Gallipoli, the unditching gear being broken whilst in use. F. 49 later attempted to tow F. 45 out, but failed. The officer in charge being a casualty by this time, also four of his crew, the guns were removed, and taken on board F. 49.

F. 46. "Fay."

Proceeded at zero, and finding the infantry held up in shell-holes, advanced in front of the infantry under heavy machine-gun fire. The Tank was in action at once, and one A.P. bullet penetrated the driver's flap, but did not hit any of the crew. The infantry failing to advance, the section commander ordered the Tank to return to the infantry. Fire was kept up, and when level with the infantry the Tank became ditched, and could not be unditched owing to heavy fire. The undamaged guns were removed, and the officer and crew crawled in the direction taken by the infantry, who had retired in the meantime. The enemy overtook the officers and crew; the crew commander was spoken to by a German, who waved back to the enemy lines. They, however, got into a shell-hole, where they remained until dark, and then came into our lines. Both officers and two of the crew were wounded, and one killed.

F. 47. "Foam."

At 3.40 A.M., whilst lined up at the starting-point, received a direct hit in rear of the left sponson, which

THIRD BATTLE OF YPRES 39

was smashed. Moved at zero, and after 50 yards received another direct hit, wounding officer and five members of the crew. The officer ordered the Tank to be cleared, and guns removed.

F. 48. " Fiara."

Received a direct hit before zero, but did not damage mechanism. Started at zero, and became ditched, and owing to the unditching gear being shot away, used unditching gear from F. 47. Proceeded to dig out, and Tank moved at 8 A.M. Received orders to return to Company rallying-point. G.O.C. 184th Brigade required another Tank, as Pond Farm was still holding out, so a fresh crew was put on board at 11 A.M. Proceeded by road to Spree Farm and thence by Capricorn Reserve to neighbourhood of Pond Farm. One machine gun put out of action there, and various groups of the enemy, in shell-holes, accounted for. A heavy fire from machine guns and rifles, with A.P. bullets, was kept on the Tank without effect. Pond Farm was under heavy shell fire the whole time, and so after about two hours the Tank was brought back to the Company rallying-point, after the infantry had established themselves. There were no casualties.

F. 49. " Fairy."

Proceeded at zero, and came under heavy machine-gun fire before crossing our front line to Somme. Fire opened after crossing our line, and all guns directed to the right, where fire seemed heaviest. Reached Gallipoli. F. 45, being in difficulties, was approached, and an attempt made to unditch, but unsuccessful. Officer wounded, and crew taken on board. Under heavy fire, during this time, from machine guns and snipers. The infantry having started to dig in there, the Colonel of the 1/2nd Ox. and Bucks. was asked if he required further assistance. He asked for three Lewis guns,

40 THE SIXTH TANK BATTALION

which were handed over to him in exchange for a receipt. Whilst returning, close to Spree Farm, a direct hit was received on the front right-hand side, while ditched. The Tank started sinking, and the water was over the floor-boards. The officer ordered the wounded of F. 45 to be removed, and Tank left. The officer and two of this crew, Tank F. 49, were wounded.

Casualties. The following officer and other ranks were killed in action August 22, 1917 :

   2nd Lieut. S. C. Harding, M.M.
   69524 Lance-Corporal Braedy, E.
   69551 Corporal Rea, R. H. R.
   69609 Gunner Johnson, W. T.

The following officers and other ranks were wounded in action August 22, 1917 :

   Captain D. H. Richardson.
   Captain A. E. Arnold, M.C. (taken prisoner).
   2nd Lieut. G. Hill, D.C.M.
   ,, H. Pearson.
   ,, F. Harris.
   ,, A. W. Peters.
   ,, G. H. Brooks.
   ,, E. P. Ireland.
   69603 Gunner Thompson, A.
   69590 ,, Cotterell, E. E.
   69523 ,, Cole, C.
   69445 ,, Polkinghorne, W. E.
   69499 ,, Bush, F. W.
   69646 Lance-Corporal Nicholson, C.
   69512 Gunner Fluck, M. W.
   69483 ,, Dennis, E.
    44 Corporal Burt, H. L.
   69685 Gunner Millar, P.
   78690 Sergeant Missen, R. F.
   69726 Corporal Calton, E. L.

THIRD BATTLE OF YPRES 41

69624 Gunner Godfrey, E.
69629 ,, Hayton, E. W.
69571 ,, Budd, P. E.
69608 ,, Hodgson, E.
1407 Sergeant Dudley, T. J.
69577 Gunner Salt, J. R.
92350 ,, Skeeles, J. G.
69459 ,, Long, J.
69562 ,, Taylor, J.
69538 ,, Anstey, J. T.
69645 ,, Harris, W.
69565 ,, Teague, S.
69492 ,, Bradley, T. C.
69480 ,, Adams, W. C.
69591 Lance-Corporal Cook, F. H.
69528 ,, Spearing, W. T.
69463 Gunner Arthurs, F. C.
69575 ,, Morrey, W.

The following other ranks were wounded and taken prisoners :

69522 Gunner Johnson, F. P.
69430 ,, Hanna, S.
69477 ,, Wild, G. F.
69684 ,, Francey, A.
69617 ,, Croxton, J.

The following Honours and Awards were granted : Honours

Bar to M.C.
Captain G. P. Voss, M.C.

Military Cross.
Captain D. H. Richardson.
2nd Lieut. G. Hill, D.C.M.
,, E. P. Ireland.

Belgique Croix de Guerre.
Captain D. H. Richardson.

Distinguished Conduct Medal.

1407 Sergeant Dudley, T. J.
78690 Gunner Missen, R. F.
69575 ,, Morrey, W.
69647 ,, Breakey, W.

Military Medal.

69726 Corporal Calton, E. L.
69629 Gunner Hayton, E. W.
69463 ,, Arthurs, F. C.
69571 ,, Budd, P. E.
69468 ,, Binley, J. H.

Belgique Croix de Guerre.

69597 Gunner Trew, A. L.

On August 22 the four Tanks of No. 12 Section, and Supply Tanks, were moved to St. Jean to be in readiness, but in the end were not ordered for action.

The two Tanks, from No. 9 and 10 Sections, and No. 12 Section were parked at St. Jean with the Supply Tanks.

During the month of August the woods in the neighbourhood of La Louvie were continuously bombed by the enemy planes.

On August 31 orders were given that the Tanks were to return to Oosthoek Wood. The first stage was completed, and the Tanks parked for the night under a guard at Brielen, finally reaching Oosthoek Wood on September 1.

Move to Blairville Area. On September 3 orders were received to proceed to Blairville, for further training in driving. No. 16 Company entrained at Peselhoek

THIRD BATTLE OF YPRES

on September 6, and arrived at Beaumetz, trekking from there to Blairville Wood, where Tanks were camouflaged. On September 13 18 Company and B.H.Q. entrained at Peselhoek, the Tank train having previously entrained the Tanks at Oosthoek Wood. The train left Peselhoek at 11 A.M., September 14, and arrived at Beaumetz 11.30 P.M., where the detrainment was carried on without incident, and the Tanks trekked to Blairville. 17 Company entrained their Tanks at Oosthoek on the 14th, and their stores at Peselhoek, arriving at Beaumetz on the 16th. The last in the Battalion to leave the Ypres Salient were the Supply Tanks. These entrained at Oosthoek on September 16, and arrived at Beaumetz on the 17th.

CHAPTER IV

REFITTING AND TRAINING BEFORE CAMBRAI

Training at Blairville.
THE site chosen for the camp at Blairville was very different from that at La Louvie. Instead of low-lying woods of young oaks, there was a good stretch of moorland, once arable land, between the villages of Blairville and Bretencourt.

The German front line had run along the crest of the Hill, in front of Blairville, whilst the British Line had been in the valley in front of Bretencourt. The main road ran through both systems, across what had once been " No Man's Land."

The camp itself was pitched on good turf, on both sides of the main road, the Battalion headquarters and equipment stores being at the roadside, or either side, whilst the men's lines were on either side of a broad central path. The Tanks were parked and camouflaged in the ruins of Blairville itself under an officer's guard.

On September 19 a party proceeded to Erin to draw new Tanks to replace the casualties of

TRAINING BEFORE CAMBRAI 45

the Ypres battles, thus making the Battalion up to fighting strength.

Life down at the camp proceeded normally, the sections training reinforcements in squad drill, Lewis guns, and other classes.

The workshop personnel, assisted by the crews, started a systematic overhaul of all the Tanks. The Tanks were jacked up on sleepers, the tracks broken, and the mud of Flanders scraped out from the rollers and switches. Those Tanks not on the stocks went out daily under their section officers, training the drivers and crews. Great attention was paid to getting the men to use their judgment in the choice of ground, when wanting to cross a trench system. On the maintenance and mechanical side the object aimed at was to get the men to rely more on themselves for mechanical adjustments and maintenance, so that the workshops were only called upon to help on work of the most technical character.

Towards the end of September rumours became current that the Battalion would return to Auchy-les-Hesdin. Other rumours said that there was a show on with the Canadians.

On the 30th of September the Battalion entertained a number of the staff, officers, and men of the 6th Canadian Brigade, with whom it was thought we would operate. Demonstrations were given in climbing steep banks, and dropping down stiff gradients. The chief obstacle in the projected operations was the railway embankment at Lens. The Canadians were very pleased with the demonstrations, the men joy-riding on top, whilst the Tanks climbed up and down the steep banks. On October 9 news came that the operations were indefinitely postponed. The training continued until a very high standard of driving and mechanical efficiency was attained.

On October 15 the Battalion was ordered to move to Auchy-les-Hesdin, and hand over the camp to " I " Battalion.

<small>Move to Auchy-les-Hesdin.</small>

With the exception of the train which was to take away the Supply Tanks crashing into the ramp at Beaumetz, the move to Auchy was made without incident. The crews by this time were accustomed to the business of entraining, and it made little difference whether it was by night or by day. Moreover, the men had become accustomed to making themselves comfortable at night in the train. On arrival at Erin the Supply Tanks were handed in, but the Fighting Tanks trekked to the old Tankodrome at Auchy.

By October 25 the whole Battalion had arrived complete with Tanks and stores at Auchy-les-Hesdin, and had settled into billets. All ranks were pleased to get back into good billets, and were prepared to make themselves comfortable for the winter. Preparations had

TRAINING BEFORE CAMBRAI 47

been made in advance to repair some of the billets, and to allow the whole of the Battalion to mess together, in one large hall. Good officers' messes had also been built. At the same time crews started to overhaul and repaint their Tanks, in the same way as they had done before the Battle of Ypres, when last at Auchy.

At this time the formation of the sections and Companies was altered. Instead of three fighting sections, each of four Tanks, and one supply section to each Company, there were four fighting sections, each of three Tanks; the question of supplies being under Battalion arrangements. *Change in Organisation of Companies.*

A trial was held to ascertain to what extent the crews had profited by the autumn training, a certain time being allowed to break tracks, and change sprockets and pinions. The test was passed very satisfactorily by all Companies.

The life of the Battalion during the first weeks of November was extremely quiet, the time being devoted to training, improvements to winter quarters, and the arrangement of a concert party under Captain D. H. Richardson, M.C., and 2nd Lieut. A. H. C. Borger.

A fresh idea in the training of Tanks was introduced at this time. Six Tanks were sent to Eclimeux to train with the 12th Division, and to clear passages through barbed wire by dragging with grappling irons and steel cables. *Training with 12th Division.*

48 THE SIXTH TANK BATTALION

Fascines.

During this period the Battalion also made the acquaintance of the famous fascine, which we were to use in the coming Battle of Cambrai. Officers from central workshops came round to the Tankodrome to instruct the crews in the art of hoisting the huge bundles of brushwood without getting crushed or damaged. The idea of this contrivance was to give the tail of the Tank some support when crossing extra wide trenches, such as were supposed to exist in the Hindenburg Line.

Towards the middle of November disturbing rumours were abroad that the Battalion was going down to Bray-sur-Somme for fourteen days' intensive training, prior to going into winter training. The prophets were quite sure that we were coming back to Auchy to eat our Christmas dinners.

On November 13, 18 Company made the first move, trekking from Auchy to Erin, ready for entraining at Erin, for our unknown destination.

Trek to Erin.

On the 14th, 16 and 17 Companies trekked to Erin, and the whole three Companies entrained on three trains the same day.

That night, about 8 p.m., the train conveying 18 Company met with an accident at the horseshoe bend in the line between Bray-sur-Somme and Le Plateau Junction. One of the trucks carrying the majority of the men of No. 12 Section jumped the rails at the head of the bend, and

TRAINING BEFORE CAMBRAI 49

after jolting along for some distance overturned, shooting the men under the other wagons, and causing several casualties. Sergt. Sutton and Cpl. Hicks were killed, and eight other ranks injured. The killed and injured were, after some difficulty, got out of the wreckage and medical aid secured for the injured.

Next day found the whole Battalion assembled at Le Plateau, each Company in its own train. The day was spent in getting ammunition and stores aboard the trains and getting the fascines, which had been put on the trucks at central workshops, into position for conveying on top of the cab. As soon as it was dusk the trains left for the various detraining points. "F" Battalion detrained at Heudicourt, and the spare Tanks of the Battalion at Sorrel. Le Plateau.

The first stage of the approach march was from Heudicourt to Gouzeaucourt, whilst the spare Tanks went to Dessart Wood, where the crews continued to work on them. Approach March.

The three Companies of Fighting Tanks arrived at Gouzeaucourt about an hour before dawn, and straightway commenced to camouflage themselves under the ruins, which were all the Huns had left of this village. Gouzeaucourt, before the Hun retreat in the spring of 1917, was a village of considerable size, with a number of shops, but in November 1917 it was nothing but ruins; indeed it was impossible to find a

E

house which would serve as a billet. The strictest precautions were taken against discovery. No one was allowed to prowl about during the daytime, and the camouflage of the Tanks was kept intact until dusk, when the work of fixing spuds and getting the fascines into battle position began. At night no fires and lights were allowed. Of course, by this time, every one realised we were in for the most intensified form of training.

During the next two days reconnaissance was made to the front line, and the final preparations for action completed.

Final Instructions.
On the afternoon of November 19, Lieut.-Colonel F. Summers, D.S.O., D.S.C., visited the three Companies, and gave a short outline of the scheme and plan of operations. Maps were given out, and the C.O. wished every one the best of luck. Just before this the Special Order of the Day, by Brigadier-General H. J. Elles, D.S.O., calling upon the Tank Corps for their best efforts, was issued.

As soon as darkness permitted the R.O.'s taped the last stages of the approach march, and marked each Tank's position at the jumping-off point.

At about 9 P.M. on Monday night, November 19, the Battalion moved out of the various hiding-places and commenced the final approach march. All the Companies were in position by 3 A.M., and were soon joined by the infantry, who had to go over the top with them.

In this action the Unicorn formation was adopted for the first time. Each section of three Tanks was formed up in an equilateral triangle, the apex pointing towards the objective. The two rear Tanks, each taking over with them a platoon of infantry in snake formation, followed at a safe distance.

About an hour before starting, rum was sent round, and each man was given a small tot, sufficient to warm him, as the cold of the early morning was intense. The Company commanders visited their Tanks just before zero, and wished everybody good luck, and assured them that it was to be " a walk over." The Tanks cranked up engines at 5 A.M., and at 6.10 A.M. started to cover the remaining distance to the front line, followed by the infantry. The barrage came down at 6.20 and the Battalion was well into the Battle of Cambrai, which was to start a new era in the history of the war. Certain it is we had the finest day it is possible for any unit to have in battle. One Company commander described it as the " happiest day of my life."

CHAPTER V

CAMBRAI

BEFORE going further into the details of the series of battles before Cambrai, it will be as well to give an account of the general plan and the aim of the operations.

General plan and aim of Operations.
Generally, the aim of the operations was to break through the German defences between the Canal de l'Escaut at Banteux and the Canal du Nord, west of Havrincourt, and to pass the cavalry through the gap thus made, with a view to operating in a north-easterly direction.

The success of the operations depended upon our ability to seize the crossing over the Canal de l'Escaut at Masnières and Marcoing, break through the Masnières–Beaurevoir wire, and pass the cavalry through before the enemy could bring up his divisions to counter-attack or organise a new defensive system.

There was no preliminary bombardment, but at zero hour the artillery opened an intense bombardment on the enemy's front line and

CAMBRAI 53

battery positions. Throughout the engagement the artillery bombardment leapt from one line of defence to another as the attack advanced. Intense counter-battery work was carried out the whole time.

Tanks advanced in front of the infantry the whole way, making passages for them through the wire by crushing it down, and assisted the advance by replacing the barrage with fire from their Lewis gun and 6-pounders.

The 3rd Tank Brigade were on the extreme right of the line of battle, " C " Battalion lying up at Villers Guislain on the right, " F " Battalion at Gouzeaucourt in the centre, " I " Battalion 200 yards west of Gouzeaucourt, along a bank, on the left. " C " Battalion on the right operated with the 35th and 37th Infantry Brigades, 12th Division. " F " Battalion in the centre operated with the 36th Infantry Brigade, whilst " I " Battalion, on the left, operated with the 59th and 61st Infantry Brigades.

16 and 17 Companies were allotted the Blue Line as their first objective, the former on the right, and the latter on the left, of the 12th Divisional front; Sections 1 to 6 inclusive, south of the Le Pave Road, and Sections 7 and 8 to the north. 17 Company was to remain to cover the consolidation of this line by our attacking infantry, whilst 16 Company was to re-organise and send 12 Tanks after the capture

Objectives for Companies.

of the Brown Line to the bridge-head at Masnières. 18 Company was lined up behind the other Companies, Sections 9, 10, and 11 to the south of the Le Pave Road, and Section 12 to the north, with orders to attack the Brown Line (after the capture and consolidation of the Blue Line) and to remain while the infantry consolidated. The Battalion (less the 12 Tanks of 18 Company, or any Tanks told off by the senior officer present at the Brown Line from 17 or 18 Company if the Brown Line had been consolidated) was to rally in the La Vacquerie valley.

The action divided itself up into two phases, the first being the capture and consolidation of the Blue and Brown Lines, and the second the seizing of the bridge-head at Masnières.

The attack was successful, and the only resistance met with was the fire from the machine guns.

It was difficult at first, owing to the light, satisfactorily to locate the machine guns, but as the light improved they were successfully dealt with. The enemy abandoned the outpost line, and such resistance as the enemy infantry made was on the Hindenburg front line and communication trenches. The attack, in fact, was carried out by both Companies, on both objectives, the resistance being scattered and the advance continuous. The Blue Line was reached about 8 A.M. and the Brown Line at about 10.15 A.M. Owing to the narrowness of the front of the starting-point line a certain amount of delay occurred before Tanks had sufficient room to manœuvre in. The crowding was due to the fact that our forward guns were firing at targets which did not permit of the Tanks lining up in front of the gun positions.

F. 8. " *Freemason.*"
F. 5. " *Fervent.*"
F. 1. " *Firespite II.*"

Actions of individual Tanks.

This section had no difficulty in crossing any of the trenches, but came under machine-gun fire, and on account of the light had difficulty in locating them. Fire was directed on all emplacements seen, and all trenches traversed; many targets were seen and fired at. One officer and several other ranks were wounded by splinters from A.P. bullets.

F. 2. " *Frivolous.*"

In crossing the British front line some little difficulty was experienced through bellying, but small delay occurred. Several good targets, such as small bodies of retreating enemy, were seen and dealt with. This Tank reached the rallying-point in good time after patrolling the Brown Line.

F. 4. " *Flirt II.*"

Caught the enemy infantry with machine-gun fire while retiring up the communication trenches. After the Blue Line had been crossed, a party of 50 to 60 of the enemy were noticed in a trench and dispersed. On the Brown Line this Tank came under fire from two machine guns. One gun was located and silenced. The other caused casualties from splinters, but eventually ceased fire. The Tank returned to the rallying-point.

F. 11. "*Fizyama.*"

No difficulty in reaching the Brown Line was experienced. Few targets were seen as compared with other Tanks. Whilst firing at a gun emplacement an ammunition dump was fired. This Tank rallied at the rallying-point.

F. 13. "*Falcon II.*"

This Tank became ditched on the British front line at 6.25 A.M., but was clear at 7.20 A.M. and reached the Blue Line at 8.45 A.M. A Company of infantry was held up by a machine gun and enemy infantry in a trench. This was cleared out, and whilst so engaged the officer in charge of the Tank was wounded. A number of snipers concealed in the grass were dealt with.

F. 9. "*Feu Follet II.*"

Owing to a mechanical defect this Tank was ditched on the British front line. Later in the day she was towed out and proceeded to the rallying-point, arriving at 8.30 A.M. on the 21st.

F. 7. "*Feu de Ciel II.*"

Ditched on the British front line but got out with the help of the unditching gear, and reached the Blue Line at 8.30 A.M., after engaging several machine guns and snipers. While "mopping-up" two machine guns were knocked out and others silenced. 1500 yards north-east of La Vacquerie village a large party of the enemy were encountered and dispersed. The Brown Line was reached at 10.15 A.M.

F. 6. "*Feu d'Artifice.*"

Accompanied by F. 7 throughout the action. Good targets among retiring enemy were seen and dealt with. Two machine guns were dealt with and silenced close to the Brown Line. Tank received a direct hit in front of radiator which also pierced the case of the differential.

CAMBRAI

After a short delay the Tank was able to proceed to the rallying-point.

F. 3. " Frolic."

Found good targets both before reaching the Blue Line, and also on the Brown Line. When returning to the Brown Line a second time Tank received a direct hit, killing the sergeant, and one man was burnt, and wounding the officer and a gunner.

F. 12. " Friar Tuck."

On crossing the British front line heavy machine-gun fire was met, but was silenced by 6-pounder fire. At Sonnet Farm a machine gun was spotted and knocked out, and retreating enemy followed up by machine-gun fire. This Tank suffered from overheating, but after refilling the radiator proceeded to the Brown Line, which was clear.

F. 24. " Frisky II."

Knocked out a machine gun before reaching the Brown Line, killing three of the gun detachment. It proceeded to the Brown Line, dealing with retiring groups of the enemy and machine guns, rallying at about 11 A.M.

F. 25. " Fums Up II."

This Tank followed much the same course as F. 24, but was ordered to patrol the Brown Line at 10.30 A.M., when it received a direct hit, killing the officer and six of the crew, at a point approaching La Vacquerie.

F. 26. " Fearless II."

The Tank dealt with the barracks and barricade, coming under heavy machine fire from its left. The machine gun was knocked out by the fire from the 6-pounder. The main Hindenburg Line was reached at 7.50 A.M., but here the autovac had to be stripped and put together again. It then assisted the infantry along a communication trench and knocked out a machine gun. This Tank rallied at the rallying-point.

F. 22. " Flying Fox II."

Captured a machine gun on the Blue Line and killed the detachment. This Tank rallied at 10.15 A.M.

F. 27. " Fighting Mac II."

Silenced a machine gun in the German front line, bringing along the infantry to the Blue Line, and then rallied.

F. 28. " Formidable."

Fired on and silenced a machine gun in Sonnet Farm, reaching the Blue Line about 8 A.M. with the infantry. It patrolled towards the Brown Line, dealing with parties of retiring enemy. Owing to shortage of petrol this Tank was not detailed for the second phase, but patrolled the Brown Line towards Lateau Wood, where the infantry appeared to be hesitating in their advance. At about noon a direct hit was obtained on the fascine, wounding the officer and the driver, the shell making a deep dent in the cabin. This Tank rallied at 2 P.M.

F. 31. " Fearnought."

Owing to fascine chain being shot away soon after starting, a short delay occurred to clear. On approaching the German front line the Tank was heavily fired on by two machine guns, one of which was at once knocked out by 6-pounder and the other crushed. At the main Hindenburg Line it took over the infantry waiting for Tank F. 26 (autovac trouble). It left the infantry going up a communication trench and dealt with the hutments on the Le Pave Road. " Mopping-up " towards Bleak House it captured a machine gun, and about 70 to 80 Germans, and handed them over to the 35th Brigade. Later five more prisoners were taken.

CAMBRAI

It rallied about 11.45 A.M., and No. 10 Section commander was wounded by a sniper when getting out of the Tank.

F. 23. " Foggie II."

Followed F. 31, getting several good targets amongst the retiring enemy. It rallied at the rallying-point about 10.15 A.M.

F. 30. " Flaming Fire II."

Silenced a machine gun in the German front line, and on reaching the main Hindenburg Line traversed along it to enable the infantry to catch up. From 8 A.M. it patrolled for an hour to the Brown Line, using its fascines to cross a deep communication trench.

F. 36. " Furious II."

Owing to mechanical trouble became ditched on the British front line.

F. 37. " Ferocious III."

Arrived at the main Hindenburg Line at 7.40 A.M., taking thirty prisoners, who were handed over to 9th Royal Fusiliers. After crossing the support line at 9.25 A.M. was called for by a party of the 9th R.F. to crush wire. Then took some prisoners. At 10.25 rallied, and proceeded; was twice called for by an officer to disperse small parties of the enemy. Received a direct hit near the idle wheel. The crew was formed into Lewis gun detachments and fire opened. Finally rallied at 3 P.M. after firing over 10,000 rounds of S.A.A.

F. 39. " Formosa II."

Cleared Vacquerie support at 7.35 A.M. Shortly after a direct hit was received, passing through the sponson, wrecking the engine, and set fire to the Tank. Attempts to extinguish it failed. Whilst so engaged one man was killed by machine-gun fire. The crew cleared from the Tank and took up a position in

Vacquerie support with their guns, and later rallied at the rallying-point, with several prisoners.

F. 41. "*Fray Bentos II.*"

Had some little trouble in crossing over the British front line, but reached the Blue Line in time to render assistance in the consolidation. Here the Tank ditched, but was towed out by F. 50. The Brown Line was reached, and patrolling done along and in front of it during consolidation, then the Tank rallied at 4 P.M.

F. 42. "*Faun.*"

Some trouble was experienced before starting and the magneto was changed. The Blue Line was reached at 9 A.M. This Tank followed F. 41, and returned to the rallying-point at the same time.

F. 45. "*Fiducia II.*"

Arrived at the Blue Line at 8.45 A.M. When 200 yards east of Sonnet Farm the infantry were noticed to be held up by a machine gun. This was silenced by 6-pounder fire, and the infantry went on. On going over the Sunken Road (Blue Line) the fascine dropped off, and it had to be cleared under heavy machine-gun fire, arriving at the Brown Line at 9.30 A.M. Later, whilst patrolling, the unditching gear was dragged off by the wire and caused delay. Shortly afterwards the right secondary gear shaft twisted, and in endeavouring to drive in third gear, the Tank ditched. Subsequently it was cleared and rallied at noon.

F. 47. "*Faralone.*"

Owing to breaking a track 300 yards from the starting-point this Tank did not start until 8.50 A.M., but reached the Brown Line after assisting in "mopping-up." Rallied at the rallying-point.

F. 49. " *Fairy II.*"

Close to Sonnet Farm a party of the enemy, on being engaged, surrendered to the infantry following this Tank. The main road was crossed north-east of Sonnet Farm at 8.10 A.M., and the Blue Line patrolled until 8.50 A.M. when it became ditched, and the fascine was lost in ditching. At the request of the infantry the trenches were patrolled. The Hindenburg support line was patrolled until a request from a cavalry officer was received to give him support on the ridge from Pam Pam Farm. Whilst patrolling along the ridge a direct hit from a shrapnel shell, which burst inside the Tank, was received, wounding the officer severely and three of the crew. The Tank was then taken to the rallying-point, arriving at 4 P.M.

F. 50. " *Fay.*"

Immediately after starting trouble was experienced with the clutch, but proceeded after rectifying the error, and arrived at the Blue Line at 8.30 A.M. Here F. 41 was towed out. Enemy were seen and fired on, on the left flank. The Brown Line was reached at 9.50 A.M. The Tank received orders to proceed to the bridge-head.

F. 51. " *Fortuna.*"

Reached the Blue Line early, and patrolled along it, firing at machine-gun emplacements. At 8.50 A.M. the Blue Line was left, and Brown Line reached at 9.54 A.M. Several good targets were seen and engaged.

F. 52. " *Foam II.*"

The Blue Line was reached early, and patrolling done. When the Brown Line was attacked good targets were seen in the enemy's trenches in the shape of machine-gun emplacements, which were engaged with 6-pounders. On the line being consolidated, the Tank rallied.

F. 54. " Festina Lente."

The first wave of Tanks were overtaken just over the German front line system, and the Blue Line taken. No enemy were seen up to this time. When close to the Brown Line a body of about 100 enemy were observed retiring. Fire with 6-pounder was brought to bear on them at a range of about 2000 yards. The Brown Line was patrolled until the infantry arrived. This Tank found much assistance, in obtaining a correct direction, from the compass. Many prisoners were taken at the Brown Line.

F. 56. " Fly Paper."

When passing south of La Vacquerie it was noticed to be holding out, so the Tank passed round to the west, visiting the four or five " I " Battalion Tanks, out of action there. Fire was opened on the farm with 6-pounder. An enemy field gun opened fire at the Tank from the Sunken Road. After firing three rounds from the 6-pounder the gun ceased fire, and was afterwards found to have been put out of action. On reaching the Blue Line the infantry requested help to silence a machine gun, which was fired on and silenced. Another party of infantry, who were held up, joined the Tank. Fire was opened, when the enemy, some twenty in number, surrendered. The Brown Line was reached and patrolled until consolidated, where three boxes of S.A.A. and some Lewis magazines were dumped. The Tank rallied at 4 P.M.

F. 57. " Flanders Fly."

The Blue Line was reached at 9.50 A.M., but on account of a burst radiator a long delay occurred. The Tank rallied later on in the day, after temporary repairs had been effected.

F. 58. " Fly Flapper."

Followed F. 56 to La Vacquerie, reaching the Blue

CAMBRAI

Line about 9.50 A.M. and assisted the infantry, and was with F. 56 when the prisoners were taken. Patrolled the Brown Line, finally returning to the rallying-point at 4 P.M.

The senior officer present after the capture of the Brown Line was Major C. F. Hawkins, D.S.O., M.C., who detailed twelve Tanks to proceed to Masnières. On arrival at the bridgehead it was found to be partially destroyed by the enemy, and the houses on the landing side of the bridge held by snipers and machine guns. A Tank was posted close to the bridge-head, and fire kept up on the houses from which the enemy fired. About 12.45 P.M. some infantry of the 29th Division arrived, and the G.O.C. 88th Brigade directed the bridge to be held by a Tank, till he could get the infantry over. Major P. Hamond, D.S.O., M.C., on his arrival at the bridge, ordered an attempt to be made to cross, but owing to the condition of the bridge the attempt resulted in the Tank falling into the canal. The bridge-head was then held by Tanks, under the orders of the Infantry Brigadier, until November 22, when the infantry took over. The town had been evacuated so suddenly by the enemy that some civilian population still remained. Two cows, belonging to the German town Major, were presented by the civilian keeper to Major Hamond, as a token of the joy the inhabitants felt at their libera-

Masnières.

tion. The conduct of the mayor of the town is worthy of the highest praise. He went from one side of the canal to the other, under fire from both sides, to warn all of the enemy's preparations to shell the town, and to give every one a chance to take cover. The wooden bridge was not destroyed, and was apparently passable for infantry and cavalry. This bridge-head was also held by Tanks.

F. 7. " Feu de Ciel II."

The first Tank to enter Masnières at 11.55 A.M. as the enemy evacuated the village, along the main road to Cambrai. This bridge was reached with a platoon of infantry at 12.30, and fire was opened. After the 6-pounder ammunition had been exhausted F. 6 relieved this Tank, which returned to the rallying-point at 11.30 A.M. on November 21.

F. 27. " Fighting Mac II."

On arrival was detailed to hold the bridge, and exhausted all the 6-pounder ammunition in so doing, and later was relieved by F. 26.

F. 26. " Fearless II."

On arrival relieved F. 27 on guard, and borrowed 50 rounds 6-pounder ammunition from F. 22. While on the bridge three men were wounded. The gears were jammed, and F. 22 towed this Tank off, and relieved it on guard.

F. 22. " Flying Fox II."

Detailed to attempt to cross the bridge; in doing so the girders of the bridge gradually collapsed, and the Tank sank into the canal. All the crew escaped without injury, under fire, through the manhole.

CAMBRAI

F. 23. "*Foggie II.*"

Arrived at 1.15 P.M. and remained until 9 P.M. on the 21st, when it rallied at the Battalion rallying-point.

F. 30. "*Flaming Fire II.*"

Arrived after F. 23, and remained until 9 A.M. on the 21st, when it rallied at the Battalion rallying-point.

F. 13. "*Falcon II.*"

Arrived at the bridge-head at 12.30 P.M. and remained until 8.45 A.M. on the following morning, when the Tanks rallied at the rallying-point at 11.30 A.M. Windows of houses were swept in places suspected to contain snipers. The officer was slightly wounded from splinters from machine-gun fire.

F. 1. "*Firespite II.*"

On arrival in the village went straight to the bridge. Later the officer and the crew took over F. 6 from 6 A.M. November 21 to 9.30 A.M., as guard on the bridge. The Tank rallied at 11 A.M. November 21.

F. 6. "*Feu d'Artifice.*"

Relieved F. 7 on the bridge, which was short of ammunition. Remained on guard there till the 21st. The officer and crew of F. 7 relieved the crew of F. 6 from 11 P.M. till dawn and the crew of F. 1 from dawn till 9.30 A.M. on the 21st, when the Tank was withdrawn and rallied. Whilst withdrawing from the bridge the officer and the driver were both wounded.

F. 50. "*Fay.*"

Detailed for the bridge, but having developed mechanical trouble broke down. Rallied on 21st at 12 noon, on being repaired.

F. 51. "*Fortuna.*"

Arrived at 12.15 P.M. and detailed to hold the wooden bridge to the north of the main bridge. Was relieved by F. 54 at 3 P.M.

After refilling on the 21st this Tank was detailed to hold the main (broken) bridge, and remained under heavy machine-gun fire and shell-fire from 8 P.M. till 8.15 P.M. on the 22nd November, when the Tank rallied about 11 A.M. on the 23rd.

F. 54. " Festina Lente."

Arrived at 12.15 P.M. and opened fire on the far side of the canal, under orders of a Staff Major, while the wooden bridge was to be stormed (north of the main bridge). Parked up for the night in the main street at 8 A.M. on the 21st November. The Tanks guarding the main broken bridge were relieved. There was almost continuous shell-fire from 11 to 6.30 on the 21st. At 11 P.M. the Tank moved away from the bridge, still having it under observation. At 6.80 A.M. on the 23rd the Tank proceeded to the rallying-point, arriving there about noon.

F. 52. " Foam II."

After being detailed for the bridge, on the way down La Vacquerie valley a sniper was disposed of at the request of the infantry. Shortly after a big end ran out, and the Tank was unable to proceed further.

SUPPLY TANKS. These were under the command of a section commander, and consisted of F.S. 1, F. 37, F. 21.

The rallying-point was reached about 4.30 P.M. The stores brought up by these Tanks were the only supplies received, as the Brigade dump was made on the road at Sonnet Farm, and was not accessible from La Vacquerie.

In reply to a request for supplies from Major P. Hamond, D.S.O., M.C., at Masnières the Supply Tanks F.S. 1, F. 37, and F. 21 were sent to

CAMBRAI

Masnières about 8.30 P.M., F. 21 arriving with the S.A.A. and 6-pounder at 4.30 A.M. F.S. 1 broke down with mechanical trouble near Quennet Farm. When progress was found to be slow F. 37 was stopped, and dumped its load of S.A.A. and 6-pounder, and returned to F.S. 1 and loaded up grease, oil and petrol, then proceeded to Masnières, arriving there at 9 A.M. on the 21st November. Another Tank, No. 6014 (F.S. 2), while at the rallying-point on the 22nd received a direct hit on the track, and also damaged the supplies.

Whilst those Tanks detailed on the Brown Line were operating at the bridge-head at Masnières, the Tanks not detailed rallied at the Hindenburg support line, running through La Vacquerie valley. Here the crews refilled with petrol, oil, and grease, and whatever stores were available at the rallying-point. The crews and spare crews were ordered down for a short rest, in some of the dug-outs in the Hindenburg system.

During the night 20th–21st November orders were received from the 3rd Brigade to send ten Tanks to Marcoing, and any spare Tanks to Crêvecœur, to attack at 11 A.M. on the 21st. Orders were received at the rallying-point, as to the Crêvecœur operations, and are dealt with under a subsequent paragraph. *Marcoing (November 21).*

The actual orders received from the 87th

Infantry Brigade at Marcoing were verbal ones, to cut the wire of the Marcoing–Masnières–Beaurevoir line from a point approximately 1500 yards north-east of Marcoing to Rumilly, and clear the village of the enemy.

Nine Tanks of this Battalion went into action, one failing to start, having developed mechanical trouble. At Marcoing two Tanks of "A" Battalion were also found to have been told off for the same operation. All Tanks crossed over the northern road bridge on the lock east of Marcoing. The bridge was mined, and the R.E. engaged in taking out the charge, but owing to the time appointed for the attack the Tanks could not wait for this to be finished. Four Tanks turned left after crossing the bridge towards Flot Farm, to work south-east along the wire, and five plus the two Tanks of "A" Battalion (seven in all) turned right to work down the wire towards Rumilly. The infantry, with certain exceptions, did not follow the Tanks. This appeared to be due to lack of any definite orders issued to them about the intended operations. Very heavy machine-gun fire, with armour-piercing bullets, was encountered, and also a certain amount of field-gun fire over open sights.

F. 5. "Fervent."

Left Marcoing at 11.50 A.M. proceeding towards Flot Farm. Caught a party of about 150 of the enemy, while retiring, with machine-gun fire. The Tank came

CAMBRAI

under very heavy machine-gun fire (A.P. bullets) from the Farm, which wounded the officer severely, putting out of action all the Lewis gunners. The Tank continued to roll out the wire. Shortly after mechanical trouble was experienced, and the Tank went back with difficulty to the rallying-point.

F. 12. "*Friar Tuck.*"

Came under heavy machine-gun fire (A.P. bullets), and at once opened on suspected emplacements with 6-pounder fire. No wire to roll down was found, but merely the stakes to attach the wire to. The infantry made no attempt to advance, and then the Tank returned to the rallying-point.

F. 4. "*Flirt II.*"

Had mechanical trouble just prior to starting, but finally got into action at 1.30 P.M. Found a Tank ditched near Flot Farm, with another standing by; owing to the severity of the machine-gun fire no assistance could be given until this Tank was run in front of the ditched Tank as a screen. Finally the Tank was unditched. A strong point in the railway embankment was then dealt with by 6-pounder. The ridge in front was next shelled, which bolted a good many of the enemy, who were scattered by the fire from the machine guns. The Tanks coming up caused a considerable decrease in the enemy machine-gun fire. Dark falling, and no attack being made by the infantry, the Tank returned to the rallying-point.

F. 24. "*Frisky II.*"

Proceeded under heavy machine-gun fire towards Flot Farm. Finding the infantry were unable to follow, the Tank returned, and was directed by the infantry to attack certain strong points. After firing at these and not silencing them, Tank returned to the infantry and took on board an officer and six other ranks to bomb the strong points, whilst the Tank stood by. One was visited, and no enemy reported. On account of lack of petrol Tank had to return, and was hand-fed through the carburettor from three spare tins of petrol carried inside the Tank, as it was impossible to obtain access to the petrol tank. Later the Tank refilled and returned to the rallying-point.

F. 8. "*Freemason.*"

Proceeded past ammunition pits, towards Rumilly. Fire was opened on enemy posts in houses close to Cambrai Road. After crossing the road, the railway was crossed close by. F.W. 1 was observed to receive a direct hit and burst into flames. The gun was engaged with 6-pounder, but no observation was possible as the heavy machine-gun fire had previously smashed the gun-sights. The infantry having come up, and other Tanks being observed to be going badly, the Tank reached the starting-point again at 3.30 P.M. and rallied.

F.W. 1.

Proceeded on almost the same course as F. 8, but receiving a direct hit low in front of Marcoing, was brought to a standstill. The Tank attempted to swing after this, but received another direct hit on the left-hand side, just by the top roller on the back slope, rolling up the track over the Tank. Several more hits were received, and the Tank was observed to be on fire at the top. No movement or signal was made by this Tank. (This account is from the Tank crew commander of F. 8, who was only fifty yards from this Tank when first hit.)

F. 47. "*Faralone.*"

Rolled down the wire to the Cambrai Road, and engaged machine guns in the houses to the north of

Rumilly. Several other targets were found in the village. The infantry followed and were left in possession of the village of Rumilly. Returned to the rallying-point at 4.30 p.m.

F. 58. " Fly Flapper."

Proceeded to Flot Farm, firing at places which contained machine guns, the fire from these being very intense. Also some were put out of action on the railway embankment. Rolled down the wire to Rumilly. The infantry were in possession of the village, but had not advanced to the north-west side of it. Arrived at the rallying-point at 5.30 p.m.

F. 55. " Fly-by-Night."

Proceeded past the ammunition pits towards Rumilly in company with three other Tanks. Owing to some of the infantry proceeding in front of the Tank (though some remained behind) the fire of the Tank was masked towards the village. Many targets were obtained amongst the retiring enemy, and at least two machine-gun detachments. Enemy field guns in the houses opened fire, and this was returned. The north-west of the village being occupied by the infantry, the Cambrai Road was crossed and F.W. 1 was seen to be hit. Shortly after Tank (F. 55) received a direct hit, shaking the officer and driver very severely. The Tank returned, pursued for some way by fire from the field guns. Mechanical trouble caused some delay, but eventually the rallying-point was reached.

F. 31. " Fearnought."

No report was received from this officer, who was missing after the action on the 27th. Tank followed approximately the same route as F.W. 1 and F. 55.

At about 10.15 a.m. on the 21st an officer of the 59th Brigade called at the rallying-point

Operations at Crévecœur, 21-22/11/17.

at La Vacquerie valley, and the senior officer, Major C. F. Hawkins, D.S.O., M.C., went to Brigade Headquarters. The Brigadier asked where the ten tanks were to replace those of " I " Battalion which were to have operated with him at 11 A.M. that morning. It was explained that four Tanks only were available, but as no orders had been received on Major Hawkins's return to his rallying-point, four Tanks were sent.

About 11 A.M. the Tanks arrived at the starting-point approximately 1.30 P.M. There appeared to be no definite order or arrangement. The O.C. 11 K.R.R.C. claimed the Tanks were his, and late for the attack, which had already taken place at 11 A.M. on Crêvecœur, and failed. He directed the Tanks to help the infantry at once, and proceed to the bridge-heads over the canal at Crêvecœur. The Tanks moved off at 3.30 P.M. On arrival near the canal bank at Revelon Château, fire was opened on the entrenchments dug by the enemy, and the enemy got out and bolted. Both sides of the canal were swept, and all suspicious places likely to contain machine guns or snipers were fired on.

F. 41 and F. 48 went to the bridge-head, and F. 15 and F. 42 to the right. The Tanks then returned to the nearest infantry, who were consolidating some captured trenches, and the officer commanding the infantry stated he could not advance with Tanks because he had not enough men, and it was too dark. He did not require any assistance. The Tanks returned to the Battalion Headquarters for orders. Here they remained during the night of the 21st-22nd.

Orders were received to attack the bridge-head again on the 22nd at 6.30 A.M. Supplies of petrol, etc., had run very low, and none had come up. The Tanks started at 5 A.M., and opened fire on the Revelon Château at 6.30 A.M. The grounds were entered, and good targets were seen and engaged. At 7.15 A.M. F. 41 and F. 42 proceeded to the left bridge-head. The enemy put up S.O.S. signals on the east side of the canal. Shortly after, F. 41 ran short of petrol and stopped. F. 42 came up, and whilst screening F. 41 from machine-gun fire, gave F. 41 three tins of petrol which were on board F. 42. As all Tanks were very short of petrol and no infantry advance took place, a return to the British line was made. The O.C. infantry stated he had orders to remain where he was. A runner was sent to the Infantry Battalion Headquarters (where the O.C. Tank section was) for orders. The Tanks returned and camouflaged in the Sunken Road. Here supplies in a gun-carrying Tank reached them at 4 P.M. on the 23rd November. Supplies were obtained and the Tanks moved to the G. C. Tank and filled up completely. During the 23rd November the Tanks were heavily shelled, having been spotted by a low-flying Bosche plane.

<small>Assembly at Villers Pluich (23rd-24th).</small> In accordance with orders received from the 3rd Brigade the Battalion assembled at Villers Pluich by 3 P.M. on the 23rd November, less the four Tanks at Crêvecœur. The Tanks rallying at Marcoing proceeded to La Vacquerie valley, and then to the assembly place. The four Tanks, as mentioned above, did not assemble till the 24th, about 7 A.M.

<small>Move to Ribecourt (24th).</small> The Battalion moved to the Tankodrome at Ribecourt by 4.30 P.M. on the 24th November.

<small>Bourlon (24th).</small> At 4 P.M. Major A. McC. Inglis, D.S.O., received verbal orders from the Brigadier 3rd Tank Brigade, to take twelve Tanks to the west side of Bourlon Wood, to assemble behind the British front line, and to attack the village at dawn by six different entrances, and to patrol the village until the infantry had established themselves there.

Twelve Tanks of " I " Battalion were to co-operate under the command of the C.O. " I " Battalion, who was in command of the Tanks detailed for the operation.

The approach march was commenced at 10 P.M. A message was received from O.C. " I " Battalion by Major Inglis, shortly after starting, to say that the attack had taken place at dusk that evening, and the village been captured, and that the Tanks

CAMBRAI

under Major Inglis were not required and were to return to their Tankodrome.

Orders were received for twenty-four Tanks to be prepared to attack at dawn on the 26th inst. Tanks were made ready to move, but at 7 P.M. orders were received to cancel the operations, pending a conference the following day. *Projected Operations (25th-26th).*

A conference was held on the 26th November at the 62nd Divisional Headquarters to arrange an attack on Bourlon Village and western end of Wood on the 27th. (The village had been retaken during the course of the night, 24th–25th November.) After conferring with the infantry Brigades it was not until 5 o'clock in the afternoon that the C.O. was able to return with the decision that a line running north of Bourlon Village and Wood, and partly along the railway embankment, and including Fontaine-Notre-Dame, should be attacked and consolidated, as a permanent line. For this operation twenty Tanks were allotted to the 62nd Division, the attack to be made at dawn on the 27th, after a short preliminary bombardment, and under cover of a creeping barrage. During the afternoon the Brigadier of the 3rd Tank Brigade went with Major Hamond to a conference at the Guards' Divisional Headquarters, to settle the plan of attack on the sector east of the north end of Bourlon Wood, to the south of Fontaine-Notre- *Conference (Nov. 26).*

Dame inclusive. Twelve Tanks were allotted to the Guards' Division for this operation.

The decisions arrived at at these conferences were embodied in 3rd Brigade Operations Orders. The operations were, as far as the Tanks were concerned, separate, the Bourlon Wood dividing the two Tank objectives.

Bourlon (26th-27th).
Seventeen Tanks of " F " Battalion, plus one section of three Tanks of " C " Battalion, were allotted for this operation.

The approach march was commenced at 6 P.M. on the 26th, and all Tanks, less one, arrived at the point of assembly by 12.30 A.M. 27th November. From here infantry guides took the Tanks to the starting-points, where Tanks were in position by 5.30 A.M., and the infantry lined up. Owing to the barrage put down by the enemy during the night, one Tank received a direct hit and had to be withdrawn. The attacking infantry suffered over 50 per cent casualties, and in some cases no officers were left at all. Owing to the continuous rain and snow during the night of the 26th-27th, the condition of the ground was bad.

The village was attacked at 6.30 P.M. and most of the Tanks reached their objectives, but the infantry failed to follow on. Very intense machine-gun fire came from the west end of the village, and though our infantry reached the centre of Bourlon Village they soon withdrew

CAMBRAI

to their starting-points. The attack was anticipated by the enemy, and the village was at once occupied on our infantry withdrawing.

F. 12. "*Friar Tuck.*"

Unable to reach the point of assembly, mechanical trouble having supervened on the way up.

F. 4. "*Flirt II.*"

Proceeded under heavy machine-gun fire and barrage. Owing to wounded infantry attached to other Tanks being on the ground a good deal of delay was caused by manœuvring to avoid them. The village was entered at 6.40 A.M. In steering clear of F. 13, which had become ditched, all teeth on the secondary gears stripped, and then was ditched. At 8.30 A.M. F. 1 towed the Tank clear of F. 13, but the two big ends in the engine had gone also. At 9.55 A.M. the infantry returned and heavy machine-gun fire was opened on the Tank, preventing any work being done outside. The Tank was then evacuated, and the guns removed.

F. 13. "*Falcon II.*"

On proceeding towards the village a machine gun was spotted in the village and silenced. Became ditched in a marshy place whilst manœuvring to avoid a wounded man. The unditching gear chain having broken, and there being a pond in front, and F. 4 ditched behind, the Tank could not be moved. Started to dig her out. At 9 A.M., the enemy being close in on either flank and in front, the Lewis guns were taken out, and fire opened from rear of the Tank. Eventually had to retire, and reached rallying-point at 10.45 A.M. Before leaving for rallying-point, handed over two boxes S.A.A. to Vickers gun team in the village, whose ammunition was exhausted. Reached rallying-point at 1 P.M.

F. 7. " Feu de Ciel II."

Proceeded under heavy barrage and machine-gun fire to the village, which was reached at 6.45 A.M. Owing to two other Tanks being ditched on the road, went left and forced way through a house and on to the road, reaching church, where infantry were held up by snipers. Fired continuously on tower until it collapsed and sniping stopped. Going left along a street every house was fired into until it partially collapsed. After this a great deal of machine-gun fire with A.P. bullets and snipers ceased. The only sniper actually located was in a chimney, which was hit with a 6-pounder shell, and collapsed with the sniper in the debris. The infantry did not follow and a search was made for them, as they had apparently left the village. Some houses containing snipers were dealt with on the way back to the rallying-point. Reached rallying-point at 10.45, and remained there until dusk.

F. 6. " Feu d'Artifice."

Advanced with the infantry to Bourlon Wood without difficulty to northern edge. Here a heavy fire from machine guns at about 250 yards' range was met. These bullets entered the Tank, wounding two gearsmen and a runner. While the Tank was being withdrawn to drop the wounded it caught fire. The wounded were removed just before the oil sump caught ablaze. All efforts to extinguish the fire failed. This was at 7.30 A.M. The Tank was abandoned, and the crew returned to the rallying-point.

F.W. 3.

Proceeded with infantry behind Tank under heavy shell-fire. On arrival in the village, fire was opened on all windows and suspected machine-gun emplacements. Went up street keeping up heavy fire until northern outskirts reached. Here encountered heavy machine-

CAMBRAI

gun fire from three directions, and infantry did not follow, but remained in a side street. After the Tank had fired for some time, the enemy's fire decreased. While swinging to return to pick up the infantry the right track smashed, so continued to fire on enemy. Still the infantry made no advance. As the infantry commenced to retire, the Lewis guns were taken out and the crew retired with infantry. The guns were placed on F. 13, and on arrival at rallying-point ordered to the Tankodrome.

F. 5. " Fervent."

Proceeded towards village with the infantry in rear of the Tank. Towards centre of village and then went to the north of the village. Nothing further is known of this Tank or crew.

F.S. 2.

This Tank also proceeded with infantry through the village, and was last seen with F. 5. No further information is available.

F. 11. " Fizyama."

Left starting-point in front of first wave of infantry. On reaching the sunken road in the village two direct hits were received, one near the idle wheel and the other on the unditching gear, twisting it on the track and the other end of the unditching rail, and also carrying away plate protecting the petrol tank. After getting the Tank into a sheltered spot, fan coupling had broken, but salved the broken parts from derelict Tank I. 28, under fire. After clearing away unditching beam, on orders from the section commander, went through village to right, ready to repel counter-attack. Before leaving for the rallying-point, handed over two boxes S.A.A. to Vickers gun team in the village, who had none left. Reached rallying-point at 1 P.M.

F. 1. "*Firespite II*."

Proceeded to the village with infantry, but owing to barricading of main street could not advance. Turning right, it entered village further to the east. It was then detailed with infantry to stand by for a counter-attack, which, however, did not develop. When the infantry retired from the village the Tank withdrew also, and reached the rallying-point about 11 A.M.

F. 31. "*Fearnought*."

Proceeded with infantry into the village. Sometime after a direct hit was received which wounded two of the crew, who were taken prisoners by the enemy, and dressed. They later escaped, and reported at the time the Tank was struck they were surrounded by enemy, and that the officer was undoubtedly killed. No details are available, as both men were badly wounded and have been evacuated.

F. 21. "*Five Knights*."

Proceeded under a heavy machine-gun fire and barrage; many targets were seen, also enemy in shallow trenches. Owing to the intensity of fire the infantry did not follow. Shortly after this the Tank received a direct hit, smashing up the right track. The Tank, which was under heavy machine-gun fire from A.P. bullets, was evacuated and guns taken out. A position was occupied in a sunken road, and fire maintained till the ammunition was exhausted. The officer returning to the Tank for extra ammunition received a head wound. After removing to a ruined building, and opening fire again, this had to be abandoned, and another casualty occurred. Eventually the crew made their way back to the rallying-point.

F. 28. "*Formidable*."

In the early stage of the action this Tank was damaged by shell fire, rendering it unfit for action.

CAMBRAI

F. 26. "*Fearless II.*"

Proceeded with infantry following Tank. After a short while, heavy machine-gun fire was encountered, and infantry could not follow. On proceeding, a wire barricade was found at the entrance to the village. This was smashed up, but a deep Tank trap had been excavated, which could not be crossed. On backing out, at least six machine guns and an anti-Tank gun opened fire on the party. Fire from the 6-pounder eventually silenced the anti-Tank gun, which fired six rounds, one hitting the unditching rail and the exhaust pipe. Whilst backing out a sleeve broke, and the Tank was moved behind the ridge so as to inspect the damage. Only a dozen infantry remained with the Tank, which was surrounded by the enemy, to whom the infantry surrendered. Two casualties occurred before cover could be obtained. After doing all that was possible to the engine, orders were received to withdraw, and the Tank was brought slowly back to the Tankodrome.

F. 27. "*Fighting Mac II.*"

Went on well until higher ground in front of the village was reached, where the Tank came under heavy machine-gun fire. The Tank appeared to be knocked out there. The infantry never reached this spot, and no information beyond the above is available.

F. 2. "*Frivolous.*"

Proceeded along west side of the Sunken Road into a village in a north-easterly direction, under heavy machine-gun and rifle fire. No further news of this Tank is available.

F. 30. "*Flaming Fire II.*"

Proceeded in same direction as F. 2, followed by the infantry, who eventually took cover from intense machine-gun fire. The Tank was not seen after this, and no further information is available.

82   THE SIXTH TANK BATTALION

F.S. 2 (*Supply Tank*).

Started at 7.30 A.M. with load of 200 gallons of petrol and 50 gallons mobile oil, and proceeded without incident to the dump, at the north end of the Sunken Road, where stores were dumped, and the Tank returned to the Tankodrome at 2.30 P.M.

Fontaine-Notre-Dame (Nov. 27).

The approach march was commenced at 6 P.M. on the 26th, and all the Tanks arrived at the point of assembly at 2 A.M. on the 27th. At 6 A.M. the Tanks moved off and the infantry followed on behind them, but in some cases they proceeded in front. As soon as the village was attacked the enemy commenced a heavy machine-gun barrage, which was largely composed of A.P. bullets. At the start very small opposition was encountered from the enemy infantry, but the machine-gun fire caused casualties. The first objective was taken up to time, but there did not appear to be sufficient infantry to attack and hold the second objective, though an advance was made as far as this, in some places, and the infantry dug in. A heavy barrage was put down in front of the village by the enemy, and after, the village itself was heavily shelled. The attack on the right of the village was first hung up by heavy machine-gun fire, but when silenced there were not sufficient infantry to attack; also there appeared to be no officers, as all had become casualties.

Those Tanks which reached the second

CAMBRAI

objectives were dismissed by the infantry, who had already consolidated. All the Tanks, on leaving the village to rally, were followed and heavily shelled, and also at the rallying-point, which was in consequence removed. At least two field guns were in position in the village for anti-Tank defence, one of which knocked one Tank out.

F. 45. "Fiducia II."

Proceeded from point of assembly at 6 A.M. and picked up the infantry 300 yards west of the village, who followed on 50 yards in rear. Machine fire on the right was silenced with 6-pounder fire. Heavy fire was kept up on houses on either side as the village was entered, and seven German officers came out of one house and surrendered. The first objective was reached and the Tank patrolled up and down until 7.40 A.M. At 8.20 A.M. the second objective was reached. Heavy fire from machine guns, with armour-piercing bullets, was met, which gave great trouble in the Tanks on account of the sparks and splinters. All the 6-pounder ammunition was expended and so the Lewis guns opened fire. The supporting Tanks and infantry not advancing, the Tank returned 400 yards, collected a party of infantry under an officer, and a Tank of " I " Battalion, and advanced again. The other Tank, however, turned back, as also the infantry. Two Lewis guns were now out of action, and one jammed in the sponson, so the Tank withdrew to the first objective (which had been consolidated with posts in front). As no further advance was attempted the Tank returned to the rallying-point.

F. 41. " Fray Bentos II."

Proceeded in rear of F. 45. A garden wall at the entrance to this village appeared to contain machine guns, which was dealt with by 6-pounder fire. All houses up the main street were fired into. Just beyond the first cross-roads a field gun firing from a yard got a direct hit on the right gun turret, killing three of the crew and wounding two. The water-cooling system was also wrecked. The officer of this Tank shot down several of the crew of the field gun, and the infantry carried on. The crew of the other Section Tanks, returning through the village, were taken on board, and also the Lewis guns; hammers were taken out of the 6-pounders.

F. 42. " Faun."

Followed F. 41 till F. 41 was knocked out, then took on infantry about 7.30 A.M. At 7.40 A.M., with very few infantry, the second objective was attacked. A heavy machine-gun fire was met with which the infantry could not face, and retired. Three Lewis guns were knocked out. Engine trouble having developed, the Tank then returned to the first objective and remedied the defect. Rallied later.

F. 57. " Flanders Fly."

Entered the village with infantry close behind and maintained fire on the windows. Continuing to advance along the left of the village, the first objective was taken. At 7.40 A.M. proceeded to the station, arriving at 8.15 A.M., and patrolled the embankment and thereabout whilst the infantry consolidated. At 10.15 A.M. the Tank was dismissed by the infantry, and rallied.

F. 50. " Fay."

Followed F. 51 throughout the action, and returned at the same time to the rallying-point.

CAMBRAI

F. 51. "*Fortuna.*"

Moved along the right of the Cambrai Road to the right of the village. Machine-gun fire was heavy. From houses on the outskirts of the village three casualties occurred from splinters from A.P. bullets. Finally the village was entered, and the infantry were found to be consolidating, and not intending to advance. Several wounded were brought back in the Tank, which rallied.

F. 56. "*Fan Tan.*"

Proceeded to the right of the village with infantry in rear. Fire was kept up on the houses with 6-pounder and Lewis guns. Owing to the severity of the machine-gun fire with A.P. bullets, three attempts to get round the eastern end of the village failed. The village itself was entered, and assistance given to a party of infantry held up by snipers. Mechanical trouble developed, and on hearing from a sergeant that the objectives had been taken, the Tank started to return to the rallying-point, which was reached with difficulty.

F. 54. "*Festina Lente.*"

Proceeded in front of the infantry. A trench in front of the village was cleared, some fifteen of the enemy being accounted for in a traverse. The rest bolted and were successfully pursued with fire. On entering the village fire was kept up on the houses. At the request of the infantry snipers were cleared out. The infantry were found to be consolidating on the first objective. Returning to the infantry, it was found that they were suffering from machine guns in shell-holes. One machine gun was put out by a direct hit, and the other knocked out by a Lewis gun and captured. Casualties from splinters were caused by intense machine-gun fire striking the 6-pounder sight-holes. A spare tin of oil was pierced and set alight near the exhaust pipe, but extinguished by pyrenes. The Tank rallied.

F. 48. " *Fiara.*"

Whilst proceeding to the starting-point differential broke, and had to be withdrawn.

Move from Ribecourt (Nov. 30).
On the morning of the 30th, orders were received to move back to a position near Dessart Wood for entraining. Only eight Tanks could then be moved as the others were being worked on to be got fit for action.

At 10 A.M. news was received that the enemy had broken through to the south and was attacking Villers Pluich in force. Whilst at Ribecourt it was impossible to get in touch with Brigade Headquarters, and orders were accordingly given for the eight Tanks fit to move to proceed along the ridge behind Villers Pluich to a position in Havrincourt Wood, from which help could easily be sent to any point. All spare men were organised into Lewis-gun crews, and proceeded with the Tanks ready to repel an attack, travelling along the reverse slope of the ridge.

Many orders were received during the day, but these were all delayed in transmission, and it was decided to get in touch direct with the Divisions holding the line, with whom it was arranged that the available Tanks should stand by all night in case of being required, but no demand was received.

The following day, shell fire having slightly abated, the remainder of the Tanks were removed from Ribecourt and proceeded to Metz.

CAMBRAI

By the 1st of December all the Tanks were despatched from Ribecourt to Metz.

Those Tanks which had been left at Villers Pluich were visited, but owing to the extremely heavy fire from the enemy's artillery no work could be done.

Sufficient crews for entraining were left at Metz, and the remainder of the personnel were brought by lorries to Bray-sur-Somme.

On the 3rd of December Battalion Headquarters moved to Bray, and as transport became available the Tanks and details were moved from Metz to Bray.

The following casualties occurred during the various battles: *Casualties during Cambrai Battles.*

2/Lieut. G. W. Emery	17 Coy.	Killed in Action.
„ G. W. Phillips	18 „	Died of Wounds.
„ E. S. Lennard	16 „	Wounded.
„ R. B. Roach	„ „	„
Lieut. H. C. Keating	„ „	„
2/Lieut. J. Walker	17 „	„
„ J. L. Sutherland	„ „	„
Captain F. Sutton	„ „	„
2/Lieut. E. S. Rickards	16 „	„
„ R. Soutar	„ „	„
„ W. A. Duke	18 „	„
Captain V. Dupree	17 „	(Prisoner).
Lieut. C. W. Carles	„ „	„
„ W. Maughan	18 „	Wounded.
2/Lieut. A. E. Renwick	16 „	„
„ H. A. Aldridge	18 „	„
„ F. H. S. Sheard	16 „	„
„ R. Davies	17 „	„
„ A. E. Smith	16 „	(Prisoner).
„ C. J. H. Tolley, M.C.	17 „	„

88 THE SIXTH TANK BATTALION

2/Lieut. H. D. Curry	.	. 17 Coy.	(Prisoner).
,, J. P. Wetenhall	.	. ,, ,,	,,
,, H. K. Ashcroft	.	. 16 ,,	,,
,, F. G. Eckley	.	. 17 ,,	Killed.
201123 Sgt. Fletcher, W. H.		. 16 ,,	,,
92698 Pte. Cousins, P.	.	. 17 ,,	,,
92692 L.-C. Bellis, W.	.	. 17 ,,	,,
201114 Pte. Garbutt, R. J.		. 16 ,,	Wounded.
91768 L.-C. Empson, G. A.		. 18 ,,	Died of Wounds.
201119 Pte. Bessant, F.	.	. 16 ,,	Wounded.
201105 ,, Franks, E.	.	. ,, ,,	,,
201127 L.-C. Bithrey, L. C.		. ,, ,,	,,
201023 ,, Such, H.	.	. 17 ,,	,,
94889 Pte. Tweedie, J. A.		. ,, ,,	,,
69537 ,, Peterson, M.		. 18 ,,	,,
201203 ,, Bursford, A.		. 17 ,,	Died of Wounds
201115 ,, Hollands, D.		. 16 ,,	Missing.
95583 ,, Fox, G. E.	.	. ,, ,,	Killed.
92525 ,, Copeman, E. D.	.	. ,, ,,	Wounded.
201248 Cpl. Parkyn, M. J.		. 17 ,,	,,
94880 Pte. Day, F. W.	.	. ,, ,,	,,
92637 L.-C. Young, S.	.	. ,, ,,	,,
69510 Pte. Ashdown, H. B.		. 18 ,,	,,
69481 ,, Martin, J.	.	. ,, ,,	,,
201254 Sgt. Lancaster, H. S.		. 17 ,,	Killed.
96751 Pte. Matheson, C. M.	.	. ,, ,,	,,
91706 ,, Eyles, J. C. N.		. ,, ,,	,,
201227 ,, Shakespeare, A.	.	. ,, ,,	,,
201211 L.-C. Wilkinson, W. R.		,, ,,	,,
201089 Pte. Eastham, W. H.	.	. 16 ,,	Missing.
201049 ,, Clark, A. A.		. ,, ,,	,,
201150 ,, Bennett, H. S.	.	. ,, ,,	Wounded.
92523 ,, Muirhead, J.		. ,, ,,	,,
69520 ,, Quinn, S. W.		. ,, ,,	,,
201241 ,, Read, A. R.		. 17 ,,	,,
201047 Sgt. Skeldon, A. E.		. 18 ,,	,,
92484 Pte. Norgate, G. H.		. 16 ,,	,,
69519 ,, Reeves, V. G.		. 18 ,,	,,
201070 ,, Dimascio, S.		. 17 ,,	,,

CAMBRAI

201109 L.-C. Latham, F. A.	. 18 Coy.	Wounded.
92575 Pte. Pearson, S. J.	. 16 ,,	,,
201232 ,, San, T.	. 17 ,,	Missing.
40381 Sgt. Cameron, J. M.	. ,, ,,	,,
201177 Pte. Ruffle, W. H.	. ,, ,,	,,
89650 ,, Curtis, J.	. 18 ,,	Wounded.
201146 ,, Myers, S.	. 17 ,,	Missing.
201204 L.-C. Byrne, C.	. ,, ,,	,,
201156 Pte. Ridgway, H.	. ,, ,,	,,
201255 ,, Purser, J.	. ,, ,,	,,
92551 ,, Mitchell, J.	. 16 ,,	Wounded.
69561 ,, Houghton, J. H.	. 18 ,,	,,
92127 C.S.M. Wallsgrove, L.	. Workshops Coy.	Missing.
69599 Pte. Roy, W.	. 18 Coy.	Wounded.
91764 ,, Borrow, T. S.	. ,, ,,	,,
91886 ,, Crisp, F. W.	. ,, ,,	,,
69402 ,, Orme, H.	. 17 ,,	,,
201061 ,, Warrander, A. B.	16 ,,	,,
201117 Cpl. Ingram, H.	. ,, ,,	,,
69647 L.-C. Breakey, W.	. 18 ,,	,,
92614 Pte. Craggs, F. W.	. 16 ,,	,,
2/Lieut. J. Black	. 16 ,,	,,
,, H. N. Morton	. 18 ,,	,,
,, D. N. Shaw	. ,, ,,	,,
,, J. Black	. 16 ,,	,,
92682 Pte. Stevenson, N.	. 17 ,,	,,
92673 ,, Haddock, G. S.	. ,, ,,	,,
201167 ,, Attfield, F.	. ,, ,,	,,
201179 Cpl. Ford, D. H.	. ,, ,,	,,
92633 Pte. Sanderson, F. W.	,, ,,	,,
77365 ,, Prest, W.	. ,, ,,	,,
69533 ,, Prisley, T. R.	. 18 ,,	,,
95737 ,, Howard, A.	. 16 ,,	,,
92586 ,, Southern, W. J.	. ,, ,,	,,
69224 ,, Foulger, E.	. ,, ,,	,,
92822 ,, Cooke, S.	. 17 ,,	,,

90 THE SIXTH TANK BATTALION

201212	Cpl.	Hunter, B.	17 Coy.	Wounded.
201237	L.-C.	Goodenough, J.	,, ,,	,,
93004	Pte.	Bowes, H. R.	18 ,,	,,
69583	,,	McBride, J.	,, ,,	Killed.
69595	,,	Blackwell, C. A.	,, ,,	,,
69668	,,	Joyce, A.	,, ,,	,,
69545	,,	Polkinghorne, W.	,, ,,	Wounded.
69429	,,	Wright, H. O.	,, ,,	,,
69629	,,	Hayton, E.	,, ,,	,,
69656	,,	Sarson, C. N.	,, ,,	,,
69426	,,	Thorne, T. A.	,, ,,	,,
201064	,,	Davis, E. J.	17 ,,	,,
78684	,,	Scothern, B.	,, ,,	Missing.
201198	,,	Nash, R. N.	,, ,,	,,
201073	,,	Starkey, J. B.	,, ,,	,,
201226	,,	MacRae, R. J.	,, ,,	,,
201228	,,	Hatchard, W.	,, ,,	,,
201259	Sgt.	Mutter, C.	,, ,,	,,
92644	Pte.	Goldstone, P.	,, ,,	,,
92575	L.-C.	Hopkins, H.	,, ,,	,,
201147	Pte.	Forman, T.	,, ,,	,,
92646	,,	Pegrum, J. S.	,, ,,	,,
201170	,,	Miller, W. E.	,, ,,	,,
92682	L.-C.	Stephenson, N.	,, ,,	,,
201221	Cpl.	Griffiths, J. W.	,, ,,	,,
69282	Pte.	Harris, C. H.	,, ,,	,,
201202	,,	Tyson, E.	,, ,,	,,
92636	,,	Roberts, C. A.	,, ,,	,,
201206	,,	Smith, W. A.	,, ,,	,,
92686	,,	Bevan, T.	,, ,,	,,
92640	,,	Cheshire, F. A.	,, ,,	,,
201187	,,	Biggerstaff, E.	,, ,,	,,
201055	Cpl.	Hart, F.	,, ,,	,,
201103	Pte.	Frost, C.	,, ,,	,,
201114	,,	Robertson, E. C.	,, ,,	,,
69228	,,	Sellars, A.	,, ,,	,,
95034	,,	Wing, C.	,, ,,	,,
92673	,,	Haddock, G. S.	,, ,,	,,
201195	,,	Mostyn, H.	,, ,,	,,
201083	,,	Wright, E.	16 ,,	,,

CAMBRAI 91

92563	L.-C. Smith, R.	16 Coy.	Missing.
92596	,, Lewis, J.	,,	,,	,,
92585	Pte. Cooke, J. R.	,,	,,	,,
201323	,, Game, H.	,,	,,	,,
69536	,, Dudley, S. R.	,,	,,	,,
93102	,, McInroy, R.	,,	,,	,,
95464	,, Richardson, G.	,,	,,	,,
94829	Cpl. Thorpe, N. L.	,,	,,	,,
201054	,, Adamson, E. S.	,,	,,	,,
91758	L.-C. Miller, J. W.	,,	,,	,,
201108	Pte. Payne, F. T. E.	,,	,,	,,
201085	,, Martin, R.	,,	,,	,,
201104	,, Lea, R.	,,	,,	,,
201172	,, Evans, C.	,,	,,	,,
69525	,, Jinks, W. A.	,,	,,	Wounded.
69588	,, McDonough, A.	,,	,,	Missing.
92591	,, Pleasance, J.	,,	,,	Wounded.
92513	,, Forrest, W.	,,	,,	,,
93016	,, Steward, W. L.	18	,,	,,
92354	Cpl. Barret, T. W.	,,	,,	,,
69508	Pte. Ould, W.	,,	,,	,,
69465	,, Hoy, W. E.	,,	,,	,,
77365	,, Prest, W.	,,	,,	,,
69610	L.-C. Docking, S. G.	,,	,,	,,
69407	Pte. Mitchell, E. P.	,,	,,	,,
201050	Sgt. Dudley, T. J.	,,	,,	,,
69426	Pte. Allin, W. H.	,,	,,	,,
69479	,, Wolfe, A. L.	,,	,,	,,
201220	,, Gill, A. E.	17	,,	,,
95448	,, Cook, F. C.	,,	,,	,,
201145	Sgt. Petts, A. E.	,,	,,	,,
69432	Pte. Pascoe, A.	18	,,	,,

The following Honours and Awards were granted : **Honours and Awards.**

Bar to Distinguished Service Order.
Major Philip Hamond, D.S.O., M.C.

Distinguished Service Order.
Major C. F. Hawkins, M.C.

THE SIXTH TANK BATTALION

Military Cross.

Captain W. E. H. Scupham.
,, W. Horsley.
,, J. A. Thurston.
2/Lieut. A. H. C. Borger.
,, H. N. Morton.
,, W. F. Farrar.
,, E. S. Lennard.

Distinguished Conduct Medal.

91977 Lance-Corporal Burden, L. J.

Military Medal.

92716 Sergeant Abel, C.
69619 Private Dolley, W. T.
92354   ,,   Barret, W.
69540 Sergeant Arnell, F.
201078 Lance-Corporal Silvester, G.
201185 Private Alway, A.
201212 Corporal Hunter, B.
69432 Private Pascoe, A.
201747   ,,   Tebbutt, W.
69415 Corporal Phillips, G. W.
92530 Private Moodie, R. K.
69654 Corporal Barker, G. S.

Meritorious Service Medal.

201017 Corporal Stokes, W. W.
201134 Private W. H. Reid.

CHAPTER VI

WINTER QUARTERS AND TRAINING

BY December 5 the whole of the Battalion, with the exception of a few details, had arrived at the Camp 165 and 166, on the Bray–Albert Road. The accommodation given to us was fourteen Adrian huts, all more or less in a dilapidated condition. It was quite evident that the Battalion would be fully occupied during the winter months. The camp had to be rebuilt and adapted to our requirements, and training had to be commenced on the new type of light Tank known as the " Whippet." We were also very weak in numbers after the Cambrai battles, besides having a good number sick, as a consequence of the rather hard times just experienced.

On the 6th the Battalion paraded as strong as possible, and was addressed by Brigadier-General H. J. Elles, D.S.O., G.O.C. Tank Corps, B.E.F.

By December 13 the Tanks were all assembled at the 3rd Brigade Tankodrome, between the

Bray-sur-Somme.

camp and Le Plateau Station, eighteen in all arriving there, the remainder of the Battalion's Tanks either being derelict or behind the enemy's lines, or too near the British lines to enable them to be repaired.

First Whippets. On December 14 two Whippet Tanks were drawn from central workshops, and the training for the instructors for the new Tanks started under Captain W. Arnold.

In the meantime work on the camp had been continuous. About a mile away from the camp was an old Rest Camp, which had seen service the previous year during the Somme battles. The advance party had discovered this place on the first day of occupation. There were many wooden huts, of all sizes and shapes, in a good state of repair. These had been the Sisters' and Nurses' Quarters, and were very desirable in every way. Colonel Summers, on his arrival, went over the Rest Camp with the advance party, and decided that the Battalion should apply for permission to utilise the old huts for improving the Battalion's winter quarters. Permission was obtained, and the work of utilising the Rest Camp for the benefit of the Battalion was pushed on, so that good quarters might be fixed up by Christmas.

By a curious freak of fate we obtained help from a German Prisoners-of-War Camp, on the road to Albert. The party of Bosche sent down were some of those we helped to capture a few weeks earlier at Marcoing. Each Company built itself an Officers' Mess. The men's huts were divided off, shelves and stoves being put in. The Sergeants' Mess was improved. Good cookhouses were built for all Companies, headquarters and messes, ablution sheds and laundries for each Company were added. The Battalion Headquarters and workshops also had their quarters built from huts brought from the Rest Camp. This extra accommodation enabled each Company to have a mess room, and gave room for the canteen and supper bar.

The winter was a particularly severe one, the ground being covered with inches of snow for several weeks on end. The great idea of all ranks was to obtain a stove to warm their particular corner. The men's quarters had Canadian stoves, the messes, canteen, and mess rooms had high open fireplaces made from corrugated iron beaten out and riveted. The effect was decidedly good, although it taxed the ingenuity of the various parties concerned to keep pace with the rapid consumption of fuel.

The huts devoted to officers' quarters were allotted out, and the officers were allowed to suit their own fancy as to what use they made of the accommodation. The majority paired off in twos, and built cubicles according to their capacity for engineering, and wheedling material out of our Battalion engineer, who, as O.C. Works, commandeered all material. Officers and their batmen were to be seen struggling under high loads of timber, which would be seen disappearing into the main hut. The result was something like a cross between an Indian bazaar and a prehistoric village as imagined by Heath Robinson. The more ambitious even made stoves from old oil drums and petrol tins, leading the smoke away by means of pipes made from corrugated iron pushed through the windows or roof. The furnishing of the interior also gave scope for ingenuity. Comfortable beds were made from odds and ends. Petrol boxes were made into bureaus, writing-tables, and armchairs. Those who were fortunate enough to discover a supply of fuel invited their friends to share their fireside, and expected the compliment to be returned when fortune smiled in the other direction.

Battalion Theatre.
The greatest achievement of the Battalion in camp-building was the theatre, cinema, and the light railway. A complete hut was devoted to the theatre. At one end was a small stage with footlights, and wings, and suitable hangings in place of scenery, whilst in front of the stage was arranged a drop sheet for the cinema. In front of the stage a pit was excavated and drained to accommodate the orchestra. The floor was sloped gently back and filled with

T/LT.-COL. F. SUMMERS, D.S.O., D.S.C.
Commanded 6th Tank Batt., 26th Jan. 1917 to 13th Dec. 1917.

WINTER QUARTERS AND TRAINING 97

benches. At the back were formed two private boxes, to hold four or five, whilst an operating-room was constructed from corrugated iron. Lastly a Box Office, with the sign "Pay Here," was put up at the main entrance. The windows and the inside were decorated in a very early English style, but the effect was good. The difficulty was to find the power for this enterprise. At first it was obtained from a "Peerless" lorry, and a small workshop dynamo, but as this would not sustain a two-house-nightly show, a more powerful stationary engine and a larger dynamo were obtained, all suitably fixed in a power-house.

On December 13, Lt.-Col. E. Summers, D.S.O., D.S.C., left the Battalion to go home and take over a new command. He had organised and trained us. The Tank Corps was expanding rapidly, and he was wanted for more work with the newer Battalions.

Lt.-Col. C. M. Truman, D.S.O. (12th Lancers) came to the Battalion just before Christmas (December 19) 1917. *Change in Command.*

We were to be armed with Whippet Tanks, and in future would operate with the Cavalry. In consequence Cavalry tactics would loom large in the future, and we were to have a number of Cavalry officers for that purpose.

With Colonel Summers there went to the new Battalions many of the old "F" Battalion officers—Major C. F. Hawkins, D.S.O., M.C., *Departure of Officers to form new Battalions.*

H

Capt. W. Stones, M.C., Capt. G. P. Voss, M.C., Capt. C. E. Curtis, Capt. A. E. Start, and Capt. W. Start. Major P. Hamond, D.S.O., M.C., went home to England in February to an appointment on the Bovington Staff. Of the original Company commanders only Major Inglis was left. Major H. Rycroft, of the R.W. Kent Yeomanry, took command of "B" Company, and Major R. A. West, D.S.O., North Somerset Yeomanry, took command of "C" Company. Several other officers from the Dragoon Guards, Life Guards, and Lancers also came with Col. Truman.

Christmas was well spent. The new C.O. and officers attending the men's dinner, and drinking health to the Battalion, and success with their new Tanks. For the remainder of the day the Battalion gave itself over to Christmas feasting in their new quarters.

After Christmas the eighteen Mark IV. Tanks had to be got ready for handing in to Central Workshops, and work continued on them under wretched weather conditions. The Tank Park was two miles away across a moor, covered with snow, several inches thick. Before the work of overhaul could be started it was necessary to thaw out the tracks. This was done by making small fires round the tracks. The work of repairing tracks, and changing sprockets and pinions, in the snow, with a temperature well below freezing-point, was very trying.

WINTER QUARTERS AND TRAINING

On January 6 the title of the Battalion was changed for the second time in its history. We now became " 6th Battalion," and the three Companies were re-named " A," " B," and " C " Companies respectively. 6th Tank Battalion.

On the 1st of January the 3rd Brigade was warned to stand by for emergency for a month, and we were to be made up to a strength of twenty-four Tanks fit for action. These were drawn from the 1st Brigade on January 6. State of Readiness.

About the 11th of the month the Workshop personnel, which had been gradually decreased, as the mechanical efficiency of the crews increased, was reduced to four officers, in future to be known as Tank engineers, and three mechanist staff-sergeants.

During the whole months of January and February officers and men were passed through the preliminary stages of Whippet training at the 3rd Brigade Instructional School. Whippet Training.

Whilst at Bray the Battalion received its first allotment of leave since it had been overseas, most of the original officers and men going on leave by the end of February. First Leave.

The work of fitting out Tanks during January and February was greatly hampered by the weather conditions, and the shortness of men owing to leave, sickness, and casualties, which had not been replaced.

In the middle of February it was known that

we had been selected from the 3rd Brigade to proceed to Wailly, and stand by in case the enemy made an offensive in the neighbourhood of Arras.

The strength of the Battalion, therefore, was made up to thirty-six fighting Tanks, those required to complete being drawn from the 3rd and 9th Battalions, on February 15.

We had to be at the point of assembly by March 1, the camp of the Mechanical Driving School being handed over for the Battalion's use.

By February 15 the arrangements for the move were completed, and " A " Company, under Major A. McC. Inglis, D.S.O., moved off to Le Plateau, where it had been arranged for the Battalion to entrain. In the meantime a new ramp at Grove Town Siding, 600 yards from the camp, had been put up, and " B " and " C " Companies were able to entrain there on the 27th.

Wailly. By February 28 the whole Battalion had assembled at Wailly, ready for the German offensive should it come. It was understood that we should be required to stand by for one month, after which we should hand over our Mark IV.'s to a new Battalion, and go back to Bray, and there train for the Whippets. So certain was it that this would be the case that a considerable amount of kit was left in the Q.M. Stores there.

CHAPTER VII

SPRING OFFENSIVE

AFTER the Cambrai battles it was certain that the enemy were preparing a huge offensive, to take place early in the spring, which was to end the war victoriously for him. A defensive scheme was prepared in which the Tank Corps was to participate. Tank Battalions were allotted to various commands on the whole front, wherever the ground was suitable. These Battalions were assembled at points suitably placed behind the line, and were held in readiness to operate in various zones and areas, in either of two ways : (1) Without infantry, to counter-attack in the event of the enemy effecting a temporary break in the line; or (2) In an organised counter-attack in co-operation with the infantry to regain lost positions.

The three weeks spent at Wailly were occupied in perfecting arrangements to meet any demands made on us by the local command.

The reconnaissance officers of the Battalion

prepared routes to the various forward dumps, which had been prepared, and routes from there to the various forward positions from Monchy-le-Preux in the north to Mory Copse in the south.

Reconnaissance Training.   Each day reconnaissance officers took parties of officers and other ranks over the routes, and into the advance positions, so that the Battalion knew perfectly the ground over which they might have to operate. Everywhere, on this portion of the front, was evidence of the completeness of the defensive preparations. Fresh trench systems had been constructed, and a prodigious amount of wire put up, so that the opinion of all was that the line here would give very little if at all.

Work on the Tanks proceeded, and now the cold and the snow had disappeared it was possible again to get the Tanks looking as they did the first time they entrained from Auchy-les-Hesdin. Lewis guns were tested on a small range down by the old brewery on the stream, and the 6-pounders were tested with case shot and common shell.

A tradition had grown up in the Battalion that we should always leave billets and camps better than we found them. Considerable work was done in improving the camp. Messes and mess rooms were improved, and the camp parade ground drained and improved to the comfort of all.

On March 13 we were under orders to stand by, to move at four hours' notice, as it was thought that the enemy might launch his offensive on that date. For several mornings about this period we stood by from 5 to 6 A.M., but nothing happened until the morning of the 21st, when, at about 5 A.M., the camp was shelled by a long-range gun. One of the first shells to land went right into the Battalion orderly-room, killing eight other ranks, as follows : *Four Hours' Notice.*

92671	Private	Coutts, R.	*Casualties to Orderly-room Staff.*
201098	,,	Marsden, A.	
92482	,,	Whiteley, J.	
201160	,,	Harrison, W.	
201074	,,	Whale, N.	
69624	,,	Godfrey, E.	
95180	,,	Carter, H. H.	
69514	,,	Bews, W. E.	

and wounding :

2/Lieut. W. H. Coley.
95510 Sergeant Jamieson, A.
92530 Private Moodie, R. K.
92344 ,, Bayne, A.
69521 Lance-Corporal Doubleday, C.
201092 Private Rose, A. E.
,, Mase.

Orders were at once received to prepare Tanks, and as the Tankodrome seemed a healthier place than the camp, into which ground shrapnel was falling at regular intervals, this was done with great alacrity; the parade in the Tankodrome, that morning, being the largest on record, many finding the Tanks a source of great interest.

104   THE SIXTH TANK BATTALION

<small>Move of Companies to Boisleux-St.-Marc.</small>
About mid-day orders were given for the Companies to move off to the area round Boisleux-St.-Marc. Here the Companies took up the positions allotted to them, and bivouacked for the night under tarpaulins, or any shelter which offered.

During the next day orders came back that the front of the 3rd Division, which was in front, had been broken, and that the Tanks would go forward to attack, and hold up the enemy advance.

Monday, March 22, orders were given for " A " Company, on the right, to attack with a Brigade of the Guards Division, and regain possession of St. Leger, whilst " C " Company, on the left, with their flank at Neuville Vitasse, were to assist with another Brigade of the Guards Division, and give support to the 3rd Division. The attack did not come off, but at 5 P.M. two Tanks of No 1 Section moved to Judas Farm, and co-operated with the Infantry (Welsh Regiment) in taking St. Leger, and covered the position whilst the infantry dug in.

<small>Retirement to Ficheux.</small>
At 10 P.M. the whole Battalion was ordered to retire by VI. Corps to the railway embankment, close to Ficheux. The whole of the Tanks arrived there by 4 A.M. March 23. Battalion Headquarters were established close to the C.C.S. at Ficheux.

On the 23rd four Tanks of " C " Company

SPRING OFFENSIVE

were ordered to a position on the Arras–Bapaume Road, on the left of Mercatel, to support the infantry in case of a counter-attack, in front of Henin-sur-Cojeul. No action took place, however.

The Battalion remained in position during the 24th and 25th, but on the night of the 25th orders were received from the VI. Corps for all Tanks to move back to La Cauchie, *via* Wailly and Beaumetz. The trek was the longest yet experienced by the Battalion, but by 10 A.M. next morning, March 26, the whole of the Battalion had arrived. Fills of petrol, oil, and grease had been provided at a point beyond Beaumetz, and with one halt the trek proceeded throughout the night. On arrival at La Cauchie, breakfasts were cooked, the Tanks filled with petrol and greased up. This completed, the next thing was to rest the crews. Very little time, however, was given for rest, because at 12.30 noon a report came through that the enemy had broken through at Hebuterne with Tanks and armoured cars, and was advancing in the direction of La Cauchie and the Arras–Doullens Road. The male Tanks were hustled out, and one section put into position at Pommier, and others round the southern exit of La Cauchie village. The report turned out to be a base rumour, and the Tanks were ordered back to their parking-up positions.

Move to La Cauchie.

106 THE SIXTH TANK BATTALION

For nearly a fortnight the Battalion remained at La Cauchie. The situation was quite indefinite, and the village packed with troops of all descriptions. Under these conditions billets were out of the question. Those who could, procured shelter from the weather, which had suddenly broken, finally bringing the enemy offensive to the end of the first phase. Those who were less fortunate lived in bivouacs, by the side of the Tanks. Daily reconnaissances were made by the officers of the ground between Gomiecourt and Ransart.

Defence of Line Berles-au-Bois– Bellacourt.

On April 9 news was received of the second German offensive, between Fleurbaix and La Bassee. It was thought that another attack might be made on the VI. Corps front. The Battalion was given as line of front Berles-au-Bois and Bellacourt. Battalion Headquarters were established at Bailleuval, which was about central, and a proportionate frontage was allotted to each Company in which to take up battle positions and to prepare a scheme of defence. " A " Company Headquarters were at Basseux, " B " Company Headquarters, Bailleuval, and " C " Company Headquarters, Berles-au-Bois. The sections of each Company were given a sub-area, within which they had an assembly point, where the Tanks were parked and camouflaged, from which they could advance to battle positions, chosen with a view to meeting enemy attack percolating up the valleys running in south-westerly direction towards Bienvillers. The 13th Battalion was on our left, extending towards Arras, and the 10th Battalion on our right, extending towards Souastre. All Tanks, except one, reached their new positions.

For some days no alteration in position occurred. The daily routine, in the sections, was laid down by Battalion Headquarters, attention being paid to the organisation and training of Lewis-gun sections. Wherever possible, billets were obtained for the crews, but in many cases the position only permitted bivouacs being constructed by the Tanks.

On April 12 a Battalion Driving School was started at Wanquentin, under Captain Holt. It was evident that the Battalion would have to continue with Mark IV.'s on this point until the enemy offensive had been finally brought to a standstill. It was thought desirable to keep the sections at a strength just sufficient to man the Tanks, and to send the rest of the men to Battalion Training Centres, where they could get practice in driving, which could not be given whilst sections were lying camouflaged in readiness, within 3/4000 yards of the front line. *Battalion Driving School at Wanquentin.*

On April 23 the Battalion front was extended to the right to include the village of Bienvillers-au-Bois. "C" Company Headquarters were moved to Pommier, and four sections of the Company were given battle positions, extending from the head of the valley, behind Fonque-Villers, to the right of Berles-au-Bois.

The 10th Battalion moved one Company to the north-west of Château-de-la-Haie, and two Companies at Bus-en-Artois. The other two Companies of the Battalion extended their fronts in accordance with the movements of " C " Company.

For several weeks the Battalion was in this manner strung out in a line of sections, each one having a battle area in case of attack; the Company Headquarters being behind at the nearest villages, and the Battalion Headquarters at Bailleuval.

Various changes were made in the personnel, men being sent to the Battalion Training School at Wanquentin for Lewis, Hotchkiss, 6-pounders, and Driving courses. This ensured that the crews were kept up to a standard of efficiency, and provided some amount of relief from the somewhat monotonous life of " standing by " waiting for an attack

Three Forward Sections to break up Enemy Attacks.

On May 6 orders were received to establish three forward sections of male Tanks to counter enemy attacks, and break up infantry attacks. Two sections of " A " Company were established at Boisleux-au-Mont Station, and the south end of Boiry-St.-Martin, respectively, whilst a forward

SPRING OFFENSIVE

section of "B" Company was established 500 yards south-east of Quesnoy Farm.

A tender was sent forward to each forward party. Pte. J. H. Wildgoose was killed whilst the tenders were getting into position, and another man was wounded, Pte. W. Atley.

The life in the Battalion during the next few weeks proceeded uneventfully. Constant reconnaissance work, over all sectors, was done by officers, N.C.O.'s, and first drivers. At times the areas allotted to the sections were fairly heavily shelled, but except in the forward sections no casualties were sustained.

On May 30 the first party of officers and other ranks proceeded to Merlimont by train, to form the nucleus of the Battalion Whippet Training Staff. Another party joined the Instructional Staff the next day. Whippet Training Staff.

On June 14 the rear sections of "B" Company and "C" Company were relieved by sections of the 5th Battalion. Billets, Tankodromes, etc., were handed over by sections.

By 3 A.M. June 15 the various sections had parked up at Laherliere. On the day following the forward sections of "A" and "B" Company joined the Battalion at Saulty, where the Battalion Headquarters were now established.

On June 15 "B" and "C" Companies entrained for Erin, where next morning the Tanks and equipment were handed in to stores. Move to Auchy-les-Hesdin.

All Tanks were passed mechanically fit, and no deficiencies were found in the equipment, a record on which the Battalion was congratulated by Central Stores.

"A" Company arrived at Erin on the 20th, and handed over.

After handing over all the Mark IV. Tanks, almost a year after first drawing them, the Battalion proceeded by lorries to Auchy-les-Hesdin, and took over the billets allotted to them on their first arrival in France. Two days were spent at Auchy, which time was devoted to cleaning uniforms and equipment.

Move to Merlimont. By noon on June 21 the whole Battalion had arrived in the new training camp on the sand dunes at Merlimont. The journey was made by road, motor omnibuses being detailed to carry the personnel. Thus at midsummer the Battalion commenced again the training for Whippets, which had been started six months earlier, but had been almost indefinitely postponed owing to the German spring offensive.

The following award was granted for the action at St. Leger on the 22nd of March :

Military Cross
Captain T. K. Robson.

CHAPTER VIII

TRAINING FOR WHIPPETS

MERLIMONT could not be called an ideal training spot for Whippets, or Hotchkiss automatic rifles. It is true there was Paris Plage on one side, and Berck Plage on the other, which considerably enhanced its social value, but for machinery, and the mechanism of machine guns, the fine driving sand was a great drawback. Also from the point of view of a camp, the sand was a great disadvantage. It was impossible to find an area of turf large enough to accommodate all the tentage required for the Battalion, and tents had to be pitched over sunken pits, revetted with sand-bags.

The success of the German offensive had driven the line back on the Somme battlefield area, and the training-grounds available for the Tank Corps were correspondingly limited.

The training commenced in a very vigorous way. The following week, Monday, June 24, the 3rd Brigade Schools started at 6 A.M., and *Training at Merlimont.*

continued until 8 A.M., an hour for breakfast, and then on again from 9 to 1.30, when all training finished for the day. This enabled the afternoon to be devoted to recreation of all sorts. In addition there was the considerable advantage of getting the Whippet driving over before the great heat of the day came on. The heat inside the cab of the light Tanks, always considerable, was terrific after an hour or two's running during the mid-day heat of July.

The smallness of the Whippet crew necessitated all the men being trained both as gunners and drivers, and a high standard of efficiency being attained in both gunnery and driving. The training scheme devised laid down that each man should, first of all, do a week's gunnery course, including mechanism, immediate action, stripping, care of arms, and firing, and classification on the range. On passing out of the Gunnery School the man was sent along to the Driving School, where, for a fortnight, he was taught to drive, a somewhat more difficult job than in the Mark IV.'s. Driving instruction included changing the gears up and down, by the double de-clutching method; swinging with and without the brakes. The mechanical side was also well looked after. Lectures on the Tylor engine, steering, transmission and gears were given every day, the whole of the machine having been stripped down for the students to

TRAINING FOR WHIPPETS

see. The last three or four days at the Driving School were spent at battle practice. The man would fire a considerable number of rounds at figure targets, dotted about the range in a manner as nearly resembling Service conditions as possible.

At the expiration of the three weeks' course the man's qualifications were sent to his Company, and he was allotted to a crew, either a driver first or second, or as a gunner.

During all this period of individual training, work on camp improvements continued. The fine drifting sand was an evil which had to be combated from the point of view of sanitation and comfort. New cook-houses, with good ovens, were built on firm concrete floors. Store rooms, with gauze muslin screens, were put up so that the rations might be free from the eternal sand-blast which infested the camp. Ablution rooms and mess sheds were built in places sheltered as much as possible.

Under the Tank Corps Sports Scheme and Gymkhana, the Battalion held a sports meeting on the football ground attached to the Gunnery School. The Battalion issued invitations to the V.A.D. detachments and to the superintendent of the Q.M.A.A.C. at Étaples, and provided lorries to accommodate those members of these Women's Corps who were granted permission by their commandants to attend the Battalion

Sports.

meeting. Teas and refreshments were provided by the Battalion canteen for their guests, and the officers' messes were thrown open to the administrators in charge of the various detachments. The event of the day was a Whippet race.

As soon as sufficient personnel had been trained, Colonel Truman personally conducted Section and Company training, various formations being tried.

<small>Co-operation with R.A.F.</small> Adjoining the Whippet track was the aerodrome at Berck Plage. Arrangements were made with reconnaissance planes to practise contact work with Whippets. The plane would go up with an observation officer, who was provided with a sort of semaphore outfit. By means of this he endeavoured to direct the Whippets on to certain objects, which would be visible to him but which the crew of the Whippet could not hope to see. These experiments were not very successful, the stumbling-block always being the bad field of vision from the Whippet. That which came to be established was the great use of contact planes in keeping touch with the Tanks when they had proceeded well forward, reporting their positions to Headquarters.

<small>Move forward by detachments from Coys.</small> By the middle of July sufficient progress had been made with the training to send forward a detachment from each Company. A detachment of the Battalion, under Major R. B. Wood,

TRAINING FOR WHIPPETS

consisting of eight Whippets per Company, left Merlimont on July 18, entraining at St. Josse, and arriving at Authie on the 19th. On July 21 "A" Company detachment, under Captain T. K. Robson, M.C., trekked to Souastre, arriving there the same day. The instructions given to this detachment were to stand by to assist in defensive operations in the neighbourhood of Château-de-la-Haie. "B" and "C" Companies detachment remained at Authie, where training and preparations for action continued. On August 1 the detachments of the three Companies concentrated at Bois-de-Naours, and awaited the arrival of the main body of the Battalion.

Whilst the advanced detachments were completing at Authie and Bois-de-Naours, the Battalion at Merlimont had been pushing on with the final training. By the 1st of August each Company had been equipped with sixteen Tanks, and sufficient numbers of men had completed their training to man each Tank with "A" and "B" crews.

The establishment of a Whippet Battalion provided for three Companies of sixteen Tanks each. Each Company consisted of four sections of four Tanks each. The crew of a Whippet was to consist of one officer, one N.C.O., and four men, divided into "A" and "B" crews. Only three men, however, were able to go into action, so it was arranged that one officer and

Establishment of Whippet Battalions.

two men should go into action one day, whilst the N.C.O. and two men should man the Tank in the next action. This would mean that 50 per cent of the Tank commanders including the section commander, who also commanded a Tank, would be officers and 50 per cent would be N.C.O.'s.

Battalion again concentrated. On August 4 the Battalion with twenty-four Tanks and personnel entrained at St. Josse, and joined the advanced detachments at Bois-de-Naours, this completing the concentration of the whole Battalion.

CHAPTER IX

AMIENS

ON the evening of August 6 the Battalion started for its first battle as a Whippet Battalion. Beyond the operations during the first days of the German offensive in March, there had been no real engagement, only standing by ready for emergencies behind the line, and receiving a shelling from time to time, without any chance of hitting back. During the whole of the period at Wailly, and the three months in the line, the constant thought had been how to get rid of the slow and ponderous Mark IV.'s, with their trying four-man control, and get on to faster and more easily manœuvred Whippets.

Well, the day had arrived, the Battalion started out on a trek to Amiens, with forty-eight Whippets and a fully trained personnel. The mere thought of a trek to Amiens from the Bois-de-Naours with Mark IV.'s would have dismayed every one. But with the Whippets it was comparatively easy. Amiens was reached

Trek to Amiens.

late at night, and the Tanks parked up in one of the Boulevards leading out towards Villers-Brettonneux, whilst billets were found for all ranks in a school close by.

<small>Approach March.</small>
At midnight on August 7 the Battalion left Amiens for the forward positions, and reached our front line at 6.30 A.M. on the morning of August 8.

Before going any further it will be as well to give briefly the plan of operations and the objectives it was hoped would be attained.

<small>Army Plan of Operations.</small>
The aim of the operations was to pierce the enemy's forward defences to a certain point known as the Red Line. This was to be carried out by the infantry, assisted by the artillery and heavy Tanks. This success was to be exploited by means of cavalry, assisted by light Tanks, and to capture the outer Amiens defence line on the point attacked. The Battalion was to conform to the movements of the cavalry up to the line running in front of Lamotte, Marcelcave, and through Ignaucourt, which was to be reached at zero plus 6 hours, viz. by 10.20 A.M. The line of advance was along the railway running from Villers-Brettonneux to Chaulnes. "B" Company would operate on the north, and "C" Company on the south, whilst "A" Company would be in reserve.

Each Company had approximately 2500 yards' frontage. Of the forty-eight Tanks starting from Amiens for the final stages of the approach

AMIENS

march, forty-four arrived at Trones Wood. "B" Company were in position at La Bastille Mill by 8 A.M.; "C" Company reached Marcelcave, their starting-point, about the same time. Lieut.-Col. C. M. Truman, D.S.O., gave "B" and "C" Companies their final orders, and returned to where "A" Company were in reserve awaiting orders. When it was certain that the battle was progressing satisfactorily, Colonel Truman gave orders to "A" Company to move in the direction of Caix.

About 9.15 A.M. a Whippet going over a dud shell caused it to explode, wounding Colonel Truman and Major A. McC. Inglis, D.S.O. Major R. B. Wood then took over command of the Battalion.

On approaching the western side of Guillaucourt the infantry were hung up by heavy machine-gun fire. There is a valley running north from the river Luce, ending at the village of Guillaucourt. It was here, and from the high ground to the east, that the opposition was coming. Major R. A. West, V.C., D.S.O., M.C., ordered six Whippets of "C" Company to wheel left up this valley and attack Guillaucourt from the south, whilst three others worked round and attacked from the north. Some batteries of artillery were captured in this valley. At 11.30 A.M. Major West sent the following message from a point east of Guillaucourt:

Details of Attack.

Nine "C" Company Whippets were on the Red Line at 10.15. Snipers and M.G.'s on the low ground south of Guillaucourt. Now 11.30. No cavalry have yet appeared. 1st Cavalry Brigade north of the railway line have gone on. Cannot get in touch as too much M.G. fire and sniping north of line. We are progressing rapidly. 11.30 A.M.

Shortly after he met the G.O.C. 9th Cavalry Brigade at a point 1000 yards south of Marcelcave, and was able to organise an attack on the valley running N.E., S.W. The enemy clung to the woods, but was eventually chased out.

Bayonvillers. Meanwhile Major A. H. Rycroft, D.S.O., commanding "B" Company, detached four Tanks to co-operate with the cavalry in clearing Bayonvillers. The action was most satisfactorily carried out. The Company had now deployed north of the railway, extending over some 2500 yards. They went forward with the cavalry, obtaining very good practice on all kinds of targets. Just south of Harbonnières the Queen's Bays made a charge on some gun teams and transport. Several of "B" Company's Tanks took part. Farther on to the east of Harbonnières a considerable amount of transport was caught on the road. By means of the combined operations of the cavalry and the Tanks about 500 prisoners were captured as they tried to escape eastwards. The pursuit was followed up by two Tanks under Lieut. C. B. Arnold and Lieut. A. L. Watkins, M.C. Lieut. Arnold's

Tank, A. 344, failed to return, and was discovered next day lying burnt out. It was ascertained afterwards that the 60th Australian Infantry Brigade had been held up on the railway south of Harbonnières and had applied to Lieut. Arnold for assistance. After having got the infantry forward his Tank received a direct hit. His driver, Pte. Carnie, was killed, but Lieut. Arnold and the other member of the crew were wounded and captured, after putting up so stiff a fight that forty dead Germans were afterwards found round the Tank. Both " B " and " C " Companies, in their progress, were able to account for several batteries of guns. To assist in the final dispersion of the enemy, O.C. " C " Company despatched three Tanks to patrol as far as Rosières. Another Tank was despatched to the bridge on the railway of Harbonnières, where the enemy had made a desperate attempt to hold on and hang up our advance. The two Tanks patrolling as far as Rosières came under extremely heavy machine-gun fire, but were able to harass the enemy, who were digging in on a defensive line to the west of this village.

By reaching the line Vrely–Rosières–Warvillers the Tank patrols enabled the infantry to consolidate on the Amiens defence line. " A " Company remained, as ordered, in reserve in the valley east of Marcelcave.

The Battalion was ordered to rally at Marcelcave. Forty Tanks rallied at this point by 10 P.M. Two Tanks of " B " Company were ditched near the railway, south of Harbonnières, viz. 313 and 332. 344 was missing with Lieut. C. B. Arnold and crew. Tank 364, " A " Company, received a direct hit, and was burnt out. 375, " C " Company, received a direct hit in the valley south of Guillaucourt, and 357, which was burnt out whilst following up the pursuit farther east of this village.

Casualties. The details of casualties in this action were as follows :

Killed.
2/Lieut. H. Seddon.
69415 Sergeant Phillips, G. W.
69481 Private Martin, J.

Wounded.
Lieut.-Col. C. M. Truman, D.S.O.
Major A. McC. Inglis, D.S.O.
Lieut. C. Waterhouse.
 „   S. H. R. Harris.
2/Lieut. J. Munro.
69508 Private Ould, W.
201240   „   Russell, T.
201168   „   Smith, P.
69407   „   Mitchell, E. P.
308722   „   Howe, D.

Injured.
Lieut. J. A. Thurston, M.C.
2/Lieut. H. J. Whaley.

Missing (Prisoners of War).
Lieut. C. B. Arnold.
201253 Private Ribbons, C.
201966 Private Carnie, W. J. (Since reported killed.)

AMIENS

At 2.30 A.M. on the following day, August 9, orders were received from the 3rd Tank Brigade for twenty-four Tanks to operate with the 1st Canadian Division. The officer commanding was to meet a liaison officer from the cavalry at Guillaucourt, at which point the Tanks would remain until contact had been established with the 1st and 2nd Cavalry Divisions.

The twenty-four Tanks, eight per Company, left camp at 4.45 A.M. On arrival at Guillaucourt it was found that the advance of the Canadian Corps was to continue, and was timed to commence at 10 A.M. The Whippets were to remain with the cavalry until the latter were ready to go through the infantry, when they would advance, also clearing a way through enemy machine guns, etc.

" A " Company were to co-operate with the 9th Cavalry Brigade. " B " Company were to co-operate with the 2nd Cavalry Brigade, whilst " C " Company were in support.

The advance was postponed until 11 A.M.

" A " Company moved off, followed by " B," with " C " in support. It was not expected that the heavy Tanks would join in the attack. " A " Company moved forward along the railway, with orders to get in touch with G.O.C. 9th Cavalry Brigade, and liaison was effected at 11 A.M.

" A " Company were given orders to push

on to Rosières, where cavalry patrols were expected in about forty minutes. From there the cavalry and Whippets were to work in the direction of Meharicourt-Chilly-Chaulnes; one Tank, under Lieut. Patrick, was sent across the railway to protect the left flank.

"B" Company, under Major A. H. Rycroft, D.S.O., had been ordered to concentrate in the valley west of Caix, and move forward in the direction of Vrely, operating with the 1st Cavalry Brigade. This, however, was somewhat delayed by the fact that Major Rycroft received a severe injury whilst on his way to give his Company orders, and no one was informed of the accident, Major Rycroft having no orderly with him, owing to the lack of horses.

"C" Company were concentrated at the north of Caix. "A" Company at once moved forward, and Captain Robson, who was next to the railway, observing that the Australians were being held up by machine guns from certain points beyond the railway, crossed over the railway and put the guns out and captured the teams, enabling the Australians to move forward.

Three Whippets had meanwhile reached Rosières. Captain Horsley and Lieut. Holloway went through the village and cleared it of snipers, patrolling as far as the sugar factory on the east side. Lieut. Howard, in endeavouring to

AMIENS

encircle the village from the southern side, encountered an anti-Tank gun, and was killed with all his crew. The Canadians had, by this time, captured the village, and established their line north and south from the sugar factory.

"C" Company, about 5.30 P.M., moved forward to assist the Canadians east of Meharicourt; after patrolling as far as the old trench system, 1000 yards east of the village, they withdrew intact, having fired at a few targets. At 10 P.M. they arrived at the rallying-point.

About 5.45 P.M. a party of the 9th Lancers were driven in from the direction of Fouquescourt, and it was reported that the enemy were preparing to counter-attack. "B" Company were then south of Marcelcave, on the road midway between Ignaucourt and Autercourt. G.O.C. 2nd Cavalry Brigade sent them forward to clear up the situation. Six Tanks, under Major W. O. Gibbs, moved up to a point 2000 yards south-west of Vrely, and from there were launched in the direction of Fouquescourt, across the open country of standing corn, in which were hidden several enemy machine guns, which were holding up the Canadians. Several of these were located and the crews destroyed or driven off. The enemy were holding a part of the old trench system 2000 yards north-west of Fouquescourt in some strength, and against them Lieutenants Groutage and Bennett advanced,

Action near Vrely.

causing some to retire and killing others. This manœuvre enabled some the Canadians to advance to a position in which they remained during the night. Both Lieutenants Groutage and Bennett's Tanks received direct hits, the crew of the latter being now missing; but the crew of the former, getting his guns out, were able to get away. Tank No. 282 stopped owing to engine trouble and the crew and guns taken off by another Tank.

As it was becoming dark the Tanks were then withdrawn, and returned to the rallying-point.

The following numbers of Tanks rallied at the rallying-point.

"A" Company, 7. "B" Company, 5. "C" Company, 8.

The details of Tanks which did not rally are as follows :

"A" Company. 365. Direct hit, and burnt out, with Lieut. Howard and driver killed; gunner wounded.

"B" Company. 359. Direct hit, and burnt out, with Lieut. Bennett and crew missing.

348. Direct hit.

288. Developed autovac trouble, but was recovered later.

Casualties.

The details of casualties were as follows :

Officers.

Lieut. E. S. Howard	Killed.
Captain W. Horsley, M.C. . . .	Wounded.
2/Lieut. J. E. Clark	,,
,, N. O. Bennett	Missing.

AMIENS

Major R. A. West, D.S.O.	. . .	Wounded.
Lieut. C. Molyneux	. . . .	,,
Major A. H. Rycroft	. . . .	Injured.

Other Ranks.

92449	Private Tunnicliffe, A.	. .	Killed.
95288	,, Ashmore, W.	. . .	Wounded.
305497	,, Britton, W.	. . .	,,
110367	,, Moore, J.	. . .	,,
201067	Lance-Corporal Crossley, B.	. .	,,
92352	Private Corby, J.	. . .	Missing.
306138	,, Hayes, G.	. . .	,,
92694	,, Buckley, C.	. . .	,,
201096	,, White, F. C.	. . .	Wounded.

On the third day of the battle a composite Company of fourteen Tanks was formed under the command of Major R. A. West, D.S.O. The Tanks were drawn from the Companies as follows:

"A" Company, 5. "B" Company, 5. "C" Company, 4.

August 10. The Company was placed at the disposal of the 3rd Cavalry Division, and were ordered to assist the 6th Cavalry Brigade, who were held up by machine-gun fire from Parvillers. The Whippets proceeded to a point half-a-mile north of Folies, on the Folies–Warvillers Road, and there awaited orders from the 6th Cavalry Brigade. The Whippets were divided into two composite sections: seven Whippets, under Captain J. A. Renwick, were sent north through the south end of Rouvroy and thence south-east along the track from Rick to Point 101; the remaining seven Tanks, under Captain Chapman, proceeded by track to Le Quesnoy.

The seven Tanks under Captain Renwick were shelled when moving up the track at Rick, and Captain Farrar's Tank was hit in the right track, one man being severely wounded. This Tank eventually reached the rallying-point. The remaining six pressed forward, and eventually reached the old Somme trench system. These trenches were very much overgrown and in a treacherous condition. In endeavouring to get across this system they all became ditched, three of them afterwards received direct hits. Lieut. A. Ryrie was wounded mortally whilst getting outside his Tank to clear away the tarpaulin which had fallen in front of the driver's loop-hole. He died almost immediately. The crew of this Tank got the Tank out after their officer's death, but it eventually became hopelessly ditched.

On reaching Le Quesnoy with his seven Whippets, Captain Chapman went forward on foot, and found it was not practical to advance along the Parvillers Road, as the enemy had two field guns, which were able to fire at point-blank range on the Tanks advancing farther.

The crews of the Tanks had, meanwhile, taken up positions with their Hotchkiss guns. At dusk the crews from the Tanks which had become ditched were withdrawn, and the remainder rallied at a point west of Le Quesnel.

The following Tanks rallied at the rallying-point :

AMIENS

"A" Company 2, "B" Company 1, "C" Company 4.

The details of the Tanks which did not rally are as follows :

"A" Company. 343. Direct hit, Lieut. Ryrie killed, and crew wounded.
354. Direct hit.
342. Direct hit.
"B" Company. 367, 257, 352, 282. Direct hits.

The casualties were as follows : *Casualties.*

Lieut. A. Ryrie	Killed.
201188 Corporal Matthews, D.	Wounded.
96472 Private Matthews, B. L.	Wounded.

The following Honours and Awards were granted : *Honours gained in Battle of Amiens.*

Distinguished Service Order.
Major A. H. Rycroft.

Military Cross.
Major R. A. West, D.S.O.
Captain J. L. Lees.
„ J. Munro.
„ A. L. Watkins.
„ D. A. S. F. Cole.
Lieut. C. Waterhouse.
2/Lieut. L. C. Groutage.

La Croix de Guerre.
Captain G. M. Mellor.

Distinguished Conduct Medal.
92870 Sergeant Brewer, J. V.

Military Medal.
165259 Private Vowles, P. J.
201106 „ Kerr, T. D.
111481 „ Ireland, D. M.

K

92353 Private Rennie, J.
201168   ,,   Mattocks, B. S.
69635   ,,   Thomas, C.
201806   ,,   Smethurst, J.

La Medaille Militaire.
92791 Private Walker, A.

Differences between Whippets and Mark IV.   Before going on to the description of the next series of battles in which the Battalion was engaged, it will be as well to give some idea how the actions in the new type of Tank differed essentially from the battles of the set piece type in the Mark IV. Tank.

The Mark IV. Tank differed very little from the Mark I. Tank of the Somme battles. The old steering wheels had been abandoned, and the petrol tank had been placed outside for greater safety. Improvements had been effected in the armament of both male and female, but the Tank was the same old slow-moving and slow-manœuvring Tank, with a four-man control. Owing to the enormous petrol consumption, and slow speed, the radius of action of the old Tank was limited. The work of the Tank, on the day of battle, was the final effort of several weeks of preparation and organisation. Elaborate reconnaissance and intelligence work had to be accomplished. Routes and dumps had to be prepared, right up to the final stage of the approach march. The terrain over which the Tanks were to operate,

AMIENS

on the day of battle, had to be carefully surveyed by means of aerial reconnaissance and information obtained locally. Objectives had to be chosen and allotted to the sections, and even individual Tanks. Often it would be a week's work, working each night, and lying in concealment by day, to get the Tanks from the point of assembly to the point at which the battle had to be left in the hands of the Tank commanders.

No one who had endured the approach marches in the Ypres salient, at Cambrai, and again the German spring offensive, could fail to contrast the features of the old type with the new mobile and comparatively fast Whippets.

The Whippets were intended to assist the cavalry, just as the heavies were introduced to assist the infantry. The great vulnerability of cavalry to machine guns made it necessary that some form of armoured car, invulnerable to machine-gun fire, should clear out the nests of machine guns from villages, and other strong points, after the heavies, infantry, and artillery had broken through the defensive system, and so give a clear passage for the cavalry to get through on their work of turning defeat into a rout, and raiding the enemy's lines of communication. The functions allotted to the Whippets necessitated that their movements should conform to the movements of the cavalry, and it will be noticed frequently, in the reports of the Amiens battles, that this was done.

As they did not operate in the earlier part of the battles, their place of concentration would be well behind the line, in rear of the heavies, and troops taking part in the first assault.

The final approach march would commence at zero hour, instead of being completed several hours before dawn. Finally, on the Whippet attack being launched, a great frontage and depth would have to be operated over, with a result that the Companies would be scattered, and the sections would become the unit. The necessity of section commanders keeping up with their Tanks, so as to direct the battle into whichever sectors they were directed, meant that it was essential that they should be in a Tank, although this increased their difficulties in keeping control, once the action was commenced, and also in maintaining direction.

The difficulties of Company commanders in keeping touch with the Tanks on such a wide front were enormous, and they were compelled to be mounted. This fact largely accounted for our heavy casualties amongst senior officers.

Whippets not suitable for Co-operation with Cavalry. As the result of the Amiens battles, it was found that the present Whippet was not suitable to operate with mounted troops. One of two things invariably occurred; either the cavalry wanted to move forward at the gallop, in which

LT.-COL. C. M. TRUMAN, D.S.O.
Commanded 6th Tank Batt., 14th Dec. 1917 to 8th Aug. 1918.

AMIENS

case they out-distanced the Whippet, or the Whippets were able to move forward and the cavalry were prevented by machine-gun fire or barrage.

The experiences of the Amiens battles must be remembered when considering the reports of the later battles.

Battalion Headquarters moved to Le Quesnel Wood on the 11th of August. The command of the Battalion had been taken over by Lieut.-Colonel R. B. Wood, *vice* Lieut.-Colonel C. M. Truman, D.S.O., on the 9th. Major R. A. West, D.S.O., M.C., became second in command, *vice* Major Wood. Major W. O. Gibbs became O.C. " C " Company, *vice* Major R. A. West; Major H. Darby, M.C., to " B " Company, *vice* Major A. H. Rycroft, D.S.O.

There were no further operations after the 10th, and the Battalion was withdrawn to Tronville Wood on the 15th, less " B " Company, which remained at Le Quesnel.

The next few days were spent by both parties at Tronville Wood and Le Quesnel in overhauling the Tanks and refitting and resting the crews.

On the 18th " A " and " C " Companies trekked to Longeau, and entrained there at 7 P.M. for Mondicourt, the Battalion Headquarters, moving by road during the afternoon.   *Move to Mondicourt.*

The train conveying " A " and " C " Companies arrived at Mondicourt about midnight on the same day. They at once detrained and trekked the short distance across the Arras-Doullens Road to Mondicourt Wood.

APPENDIX TO CHAPTER IX

Since the foregoing account of the operations of the Battalion in the Amiens battles was written, Lieut. C. B. Arnold, D.S.O., whose action in Whippet No. 344 has been referred to previously, has been repatriated, and the following complete account of his action is now available:

" On August the 8th, 1918, I commanded Whippet ' Musical Box ' in ' B ' Company, 6th Battalion. We left the lying-up point at zero (0420) hours and proceeded across country to the south side of the railway at Villers-Bretonneux. We crossed the railway, in column of sections, by the bridge on the eastern outskirts of the town. I reached the British front line and passed through the Australian infantry (2nd A. Div.) and some of our heavy Tanks (Mk. V.) in company with the remainder of the Whippets of ' B ' Company.

" Four sections of ' B ' Company proceeded parallel with the railway (Amiens–Ham) across country due east. After proceeding about 2000 yards in this direction I found myself to be the leading machine, owing to others having become ditched, etc. To my immediate front I could see more Mark V. Tanks being followed very closely by Australian infantry. About this time we came under direct shell fire from a 4-gun field battery, of which I could see the flashes, between Abancourt and Bayonvillers. Two Mark V. Tanks, 150 yards on my right front, were knocked out. I saw clouds of smoke coming out of these machines, and the crews evacuate

AMIENS

them. The infantry following the heavy machines were suffering casualties from this battery. I turned half left and ran diagonally across the front of the battery at a distance of about 600 yards. Both my guns were able to fire on the battery, in spite of which they got off about eight rounds at me without damage, but sufficiently close to be audible inside the cab, and I could see the flashes of each gun as it fired. By this time I had passed behind a belt of trees running along a roadside. I ran along this belt until level with the battery, when I turned full right and engaged the battery in the rear. On observing our appearance from the belt of trees, the gunners, some thirty in number, abandoned their guns and tried to get away. Gunner Ribbans and I accounted for the whole number of the enemy. I cruised forward, making a detour to the left, and shot a number of the enemy, who appeared to be demoralised, and were moving about the country in all directions. This detour brought me back to the railway siding N.N.W. of Guillaucourt. I could now see other Whippets coming up and a few Mark V.'s also. The Australian infantry, who followed magnificently, had now passed through the battery position which we had accounted for, and were lying in a sunken road about 400 yards past the battery, and slightly to the left of it. I got out of my machine and spoke to an Australian full Lieut., and asked if he wanted any help. Whilst talking to him, he received a bullet which struck the metal shoulder title, a piece of the bullet casing entering his shoulder. While he was being dressed, Major Rycroft (horse) and Lieut. Waterhouse (Tanks) and Captain Strachan of 'B' Company, 6th Battalion, arrived and received confirmation from the Australian officer of our having knocked out the field battery. I told Major Rycroft what we had done, and moved off again at once, as it appeared to be unwise for four machines (Lieut. Watkins had also arrived) to remain stationary at one spot. I proceeded parallel with the railway embankment in an east direction, passing through two cavalry patrols of about twelve men each. The first patrol was receiving casualties from a party of enemy in a field of corn. I dealt with this, killing three or four, the remainder escaping out of sight into the corn. Proceeding farther east, I saw the second patrol chasing six of the enemy. The leading horse was so tired that he was not gaining appreciably on the rearmost Hun. Some of the leading fugitives turned about and fired at the cavalry men, when sword was stretched out and practically touching the back of the last Hun. Horse and rider were brought down on the left of the road. The remainder of the cavalry men deployed to the right, coming in close under the railway embankment, where they dismounted and came under fire from the enemy, who had now taken up a position on the railway bridge, and were firing over the parapet, inflicting one or two casualties. I ran the machine up until we had a clear view of the bridge, and killed four of the enemy with one long burst, the other running across the bridge and so down the opposite slope out of sight. On our left I could see, about three quarters of a mile away, a train on fire, being towed by an engine. I proceeded further east, still parallel to the railway, and approached carefully a small valley marked on my map as containing Boche hutments. As I entered the valley (between Bayonvillers and Harbonnières) at right angles, many enemy were visible packing kits and others retiring. On our opening fire on the nearest, many others appeared from huts, making for the end of the valley, their object being to get over the embankment and so out of our sight. We accounted for many of these. I cruised round, Ribbans went into one of these huts and returned, and we counted about sixty dead and wounded. There was evidence of shell

AMIENS

fire amongst the huts, but we certainly accounted for most of the casualties counted there. I turned left from the railway and cruised across country, as lines of enemy infantry could be seen retiring. We fired at these many times at ranges of 200 yards to 600 yards. These targets were fleeting, owing to the enemy getting down into the corn when fired on. In spite of this, many casualties must have been inflicted as we cruised up and down for at least an hour. I did not see any more of our troops or machines after leaving cavalry patrols already referred to. During the cruising, being the only machine to get through, we invariably received intense rifle and machine-gun fire. I would here beg to suggest that no petrol be carried on the outside of the machine, as under orders we were carrying nine tins of petrol on the roof, for refilling purposes when well into the enemy lines (should opportunity occur). The perforated tins allowed the petrol to run all over the cab. These fumes combined with the intense bullet splash, and the great heat after being in action (by this time nine to ten hours), made it necessary at this point to breathe through the mouthpiece of the box respirator without actually wearing the mask.

"At 1400 hours or thereabouts I again proceeded east, parallel to the railway and about 100 yards north of it. I could see a large aerodrome and also an observation balloon at a height of about 200 feet. I could also see great quantities of motor and horse transport moving in all directions. Over the top of another bridge on my left I could see the cover of a lorry coming in my direction. I moved up out of sight and waited until he topped the bridge, when I shot the driver. The lorry ran into a right-hand ditch. The railway had now come out of the cutting in which it had rested all the while and I could see both sides of it. I could see a long line of men retiring on both sides of the railway, and fired at these at ranges of 400 to 500 yards, inflicting heavy casualties. I passed through these and also accounted for one horse and the driver of a two-horsed canvas-covered waggon on the far side of the railway. We now crossed a small road which crossed the main railway, and came into view of large horse and waggon lines, which ran across the railway and close to it. Gunner Ribbans (R.H. Gunner) here had a view of the south side of railway and fired continuously into motor and horse transport moving on three roads (one N. and S., one almost parallel to the railway, and one diagonally between these two). I fired many bursts at 600 yards to 800 yards at transport, blocking roads on my left, causing great confusion. Rifle and machine-gun fire was not heavy at this time, owing to our sudden appearance, as the roads were all banked up in order to cross the railway. There were about twelve men in the middle aisle of these lines. I fired a long burst at these. Some went down and others got in amongst the wheels and undergrowth. I turned quarter left towards a small copse, where there were more horses and men about 200 yards away. On the way across we met the most intense rifle and machine-gun fire imaginable, from all sides. When at all possible we returned the fire, until the left-hand revolver port cover was shot away. I withdrew the forward gun, locked the mounting, and held the body of the gun against the hole. Petrol was still running down the inside of the back door. Fumes and heat combined were very bad. We were still moving forward and I was shouting to Driver Carnie to turn about, as it was impossible to continue the action, when two heavy concussions closely followed one another and the cab burst into flames. Carnie and Ribbans got to the door and collapsed. I was almost overcome, but managed to get the door open and fell out on to the ground, and was able to drag out the other two men. Burning petrol was running on to the ground where we were lying. The fresh air revived us and we all got up and made a short rush to get away from the burning petrol. We were all on fire. In this rush Carnie was shot in the stomach and killed. We rolled over and over to try to extinguish the flames. I saw numbers of the enemy approaching from all round. The first arrival came for me with a rifle and bayonet. I got hold of this and the point of the bayonet entered my right forearm. The second man struck at my head with the butt end of his rifle, hit my shoulder and neck and knocked me down. When I came to, there were dozens all round me, and any one who could reach me did so, and I was well kicked. They were furious. Ribbans and I were taken away and stood by ourselves about 20 yards clear of the crowd. An argument ensued and we were eventually marched to a dug-out, where paper bandages were put on our hands. Our faces were left as they were. We were then marched down to the main railway. There we joined a party of about eight enemy and marched past a field kitchen, where I signed for food. We had had nothing since 8.30 P.M. on the night previous to the action and it was 3.30 P.M. when we were set on fire. We went on to a village, where on my intelligence map a Divisional H.Q. had been marked. An elderly, stout officer interrogated me, asking if I was an officer. I said 'Yes.' He then asked various other questions, to which I replied, 'I do not know.' He said, 'Do you mean you do not know or you will not tell me?' I said, 'You can take it whichever way you wish.' He then struck me in the face, and went away. We went on to Chaulnes to a canvas hospital, on the right side of the railway, where I was injected with anti-tetanus. Later I was again interrogated with the same result as above, except that, instead of being struck, I received five days' solitary confinement in a room with no window, and only a small piece of bread and a bowl of soup each day. On the fifth day I was again interrogated, and said the same as before. I said that he had no right to give me solitary confinement, and that unless I was released I should, at first opportunity, report him to the highest possible authority. The next day I was sent away, and eventually reached the camp at Freiburg, where I found my brother, Captain A. E. Arnold, M.C., Tank Corps. The conduct of Gunner Ribbans and Driver Carnie was beyond all praise throughout. Driver Carnie drove from Villers-Bretonneux onwards. The Tank was found close to the small railway on the eastern side of the Harbonnières-Rosières Road.

(Signed)   C. B. ARNOLD. (Lieut.)
6th Tank Battalion.

1*st January* 1919."

CHAPTER X

FROM AYETTE TO THE HINDENBURG LINE

THE Battalion was not allowed much breathing-time. Mondicourt Wood was not to be a sylvan retreat, where the crews could fight the Amiens battles over again, and give their experiences those finishing-touches so necessary before passing into Battalion legends. Only "A" and "C" Companies had entrained at Longeau, "B" Company, under Major H. Darby, M.C., remaining at Le Quesnel for future operations on the 4th Army front.

On the afternoon of August 19, B.H.Q., "A" and "C" Companies' headquarters, with "A" crews, moved to Le Bazeque Wood, between Humber Camp and the Doullens Road, where they spent the night in the Tank Camp, which had been pitched there. It was intended that the Tanks with the "B" crews should trek to Quesnoy Farm, and be up there till the morning of the new attack. It was found impossible to get as far as Quesnoy Farm, during the hours of darkness, and so the twenty-three Tanks parked

Move from Mondicourt.

up for the night at Pommier. The next day was spent in making arrangements for supplies, and in reconnoitring the routes from Quesnoy to the front line at Ayette.

August 21. On the night of 20th - 21st August, twenty-three Tanks of "A" and "C" Companies left Pommier, "A" Compány being under the command of Major F. Vandervell, and "C" Company under Major W. O. Gibbs, and trekked as far as the valley between Quesnoy Farm and Monchy-au-Bois, and running towards Doullens and Ayette. This point was reached 12.30 midnight, the crews getting down to rest by the Tanks, and covering themselves with the tarpaulins. They were roused by the gas guard at 4.30 A.M., and hot tea, brought up in containers, was issued. At 5 A.M. the Companies started for action. On passing through our Battery positions at Ayette a dense fog came over the whole battlefield. A rather heavy mist had settled at zero hour, and this had been much accentuated by the smoke shells and our own artillery fire. The fog had considerably helped the infantry attack on the first systems. But at 8 A.M. in front of Courcelles, it was quite impossible to see more than ten yards ahead.

By 11 A.M. the fog had considerably lifted, and as by this time the infantry had consolidated on the railway east of Courcelles, the Companies were pushed forward to a valley 100 yards south

T/MAJOR A/LT.-COL. R. B. WOOD.
(Fatally wounded, 22nd Aug. 1918.)
Commanded 6th Tank Batt., 9th Aug. 1918 to 22nd Aug. 1918.

AYETTE TO HINDENBURG LINE 143

of Courcelles, and about 300 yards west of the railway. It was decided to try and push a Whippet patrol across the railway, and to prevent the enemy from consolidating; " A " Company to cross south of Courcelles, and " C " Company north. Whilst giving instructions to the Company commanders, the Commanding Officer, Lieut.-Col. R. B. Wood, was hit by a splinter from a shell, and fell mortally wounded, dying almost immediately. About 1 P.M. a patrol of five Tanks, under Captain T. K. Robson, M.C., got across the railway, crossing north of Courcelles, turning to the south. After patrolling round Gomiecourt and Triangle Copse, recrossed the railway south of Courcelles. Unfortunately after crossing our line two Tanks received direct hits.

At 5.30 P.M. all Tanks were ordered to rally at Ayette. Twenty-one Battalion Tanks rallied. A. 328 received a direct hit towards the south of Courcelles.

On the morning of the 22nd, at 6 A.M., the Battalion headquarters and all the Tanks moved back to Monchy-au-Bois, where Battalion headquarters was to be established. <small>Move to Monchy-au-Bois.</small>

On the evening of the 22nd orders came from the 2nd Brigade that fifteen Whippets would operate with the 2nd Division on the following day.

The general plan of operations contemplated

was to exploit the success of the capture of Gomiecourt, carried out early the same morning by the 3rd Division and 12th Tank Battalion.

August 23. Orders were received from the 2nd Tank Brigade that " A " Company, consisting of six Whippets, under Capt. R. E. Howell, and " C " Company of nine Whippets, under Capt. A. R. Chapman, were to support the 2nd Division in the capture of Ervillers, Behagnies, and Sapignies. On the morning of August 23, the 4th Corps on the right would attack Achiet-le-Grand and Bihucourt, but the operations of the 2nd Division would proceed irrespective of the success of the 4th Corps.

The fifteen Whippets left Monchy-au-Bois at 6 A.M., 23rd, and joined the infantry on the Blue Line at 8.30 A.M.

" A " Company proceeded with the infantry to the starting-point, 1st King's and 2nd South Staffs., to the east of the railway. Just before the starting-point was reached, Whippet A. 351, Lieut. J. Black, developed mechanical trouble north of Courcelles. Whilst outside, trying to repair the Whippet, Lieut. Black and the Battalion Engineer, Captain H. Atherton, were wounded by shell fire. Lieut. Black subsequently died of wounds.

Ervillers. The plan arranged with the infantry was to outflank the village. Three Whippets were detailed to proceed to the north of Ervillers with

AYETTE TO HINDENBURG LINE

the 1st Battalion Kings, and three Whippets to the south with the 2nd South Staffs. This plan being altered by the loss of A. 351, the remaining five Whippets pushed on ahead of the infantry, leaving the starting-point at zero 11 A.M., and to ensure that all machine guns were effectively dealt with, orders were given to move on zigzag lines across the front towards the village.

The advance continued without difficulty. On approaching the system in front of Ervillers the enemy left the trenches and scattered in all directions, offering good targets for the Hotchkiss gunners, who did much execution. Owing to the efficient way in which the Tanks did their work, our infantry were in the village at 12.5 P.M. The five Whippets, therefore, according to plan, proceeded to the east of the village to give protection, whilst the infantry consolidated 200 yards in front of Ervillers—the 1st King's to consolidate left of Ervillers, and the 2nd South Staffs. on the right of the village.

Whilst the consolidation was in progress Whippets A. 287 (Captain J. L. Lees) and A. 363 (2/Lieut. Innes) received direct hits, whilst patrolling on the further side of Ervillers. Both Whippets caught fire and were burnt out. The crew of A. 363 were all wounded. The crew of A. 287 (Captain Lees) got clear of the Tank, but when they reached the infantry Captain Lees found his driver (Corporal Heddon) was missing, and as he knew that he had been wounded, Captain Lees, although himself wounded, with great gallantry went back for him, but was killed almost immediately by a shell.

The consolidation having been completed, the remaining three Whippets left and started on their return journey to the rallying-point. Whippet A. 360 (Lieut. Muir) received a direct hit about 1000 yards to the right of Ervillers, and Whippet A. 294 (2/Lieut. Pollitt) received a direct hit in almost the same place. The crew of Lieut. Muir's Tank were wounded, whilst in Tank A. 294, 2/Lieut. Pollitt was wounded, Private Griffiths killed, and Private Bayne badly shell-shocked. Tank A. 289 rallied at Battalion rallying-point, Ayette, at 3 P.M.

From the infantry point of view the action was entirely successful. In the opinion of the O.C. King's Liverpool Regiment, at Ervillers, the Whippets saved the Battalion many casualties by gaining ground and drawing fire from the infantry, in addition to inflicting casualties on the enemy.

Behagnies and Sapignies. The duty allotted to the nine Whippets of " C " Company was similar to that of " A " Company. They were to assist the infantry of the 2nd Division in the capture and consolidation of Behagnies and Sapignies. But as the operations for the capture of these two villages were to be carried out irrespective of the success

AYETTE TO HINDENBURG LINE 147

of the attack on Achiet-le-Grand and Bihucourt, the G.O.C. these operations requested Captain Chapman, in command of " C " Company Whippets, to take special precautions so that the right flank of the attack might be protected by Whippets.

The Company had met their infantry at a point to the north of Courcelles at 8.30, and moved at 10.10 A.M. towards the railway.

The intention of the Company commander was that the whole Company should move forward in line of sections, and cross the railway between Gomiecourt and Logeast Wood. On approaching the railway a very heavy barrage was encountered. Shortly after crossing the railway the two leading Whippets were knocked out by direct hits from an anti-Tank gun on the railway embankment, which from information received was supposed to be entirely cleared and in our hands. Tank A. 334 caught fire. Captain H. N. Morton, M.C., was severely shell-shocked. The driver, Private Evenden, was killed, and the gunner, Private P. E. Budd, was wounded. The next Tank, A. 296, was hit almost immediately after, and set on fire. 2/Lieut. Cummings and Private W. Gibbs were severely wounded. The remaining two Whippets of Captain Morton's section wheeled left and joined the other five, and the whole seven Tanks crossed the railway at a point to the west of Gomiecourt.

Whilst with the infantry to the west of Courcelles, it was noticed that the artillery barrage table had been altered, and that the rate of progress was 100 yards in four minutes. The section commanders reported this to the Company commander, who ordered them to manœuvre, and wheel about, and so let the barrage keep ahead. As the barrage would not lift from Behagnies until 1 P.M. this meant a considerable time during which the Whippets would be cruising about under machine-gun and anti-Tank-gun fire, waiting to put the infantry on to their objective.

The remaining seven Whippets left the starting-point at zero hour (at 11 A.M.), passing to the south of the village of Gomiecourt, with the intention of joining the 5th Infantry Brigade to the south-east of this village. Several of the Whippets passed through our artillery barrage. On reaching the cross-roads the slowness of the barrage caused them to wheel about. About this time large numbers of the enemy broke from cover and scattered. The gunners, having good targets, inflicted a large number of casualties. Machine guns played on them in great volume, and specially from the direction about 2000 yards east of Achiet-le-Grand. These facts, viz. the slowness of the barrage, and the necessity of attacking the machine guns on the right, caused them to alter the direction of their attack and make towards the right of Achiet-le-Grand. Going in this direction they cut off a large part of the enemy, several hundreds, north of Achiet-le-Grand and Bihucourt, who had been resisting the attack of the 99th Brigade. The Whippets headed them in the direction of our lines, where they were escorted to the rear by our infantry. This sudden attack in the rear of the enemy certainly enabled the infantry (K.R.R.) to get through Achiet-le-Grand with slight losses. The seven Whippets then rallied in the dead ground to the north of Achiet-le-Grand, the intention of the officers being to get into touch with the infantry and find out the situation, with a view to giving further assistance. Whilst rallying at this point it was found that 2/Lieut. J. W. Murray, who commanded Tank A. 339, had been wounded whilst guiding his Whippet across the railway. The Whippet had proceeded, however, under the command of Sergeant Burchett, who also became a casualty about half an hour after zero hour. The driver, Pte. Bussey, however, after attending to his sergeant, continued to follow his section commander's Tank, and, when opportunity offered, locked his back axle and fired his Hotchkiss gun. When near the infantry he asked an officer if he could supply a gunner to carry on the fight. The Company commander ordered this Whippet to the rallying-point at 1.40 P.M.

Achiet-le-Grand.

The remaining six Whippets were detailed by the Company commander to go into action again as follows :

Two to clear the roads on the right of Achiet-le-Grand, and the old hutment immediately to the east of this road, and the small copse situated ahead. These two Whippets, A. 333 and A. 349, under 2/Lieut. F. F. Bromley, advanced round the left side to the east end of the village of Bihucourt, where they did considerable execution among the enemy, and were able to prevent three field guns from limbering up, killing several of the personnel, and horses. The infantry then pushed on and consolidated in the village.

The Tanks then proceeded towards Sapignies, but as they were not followed by infantry, and came under heavy machine-gun fire, they returned to Bihucourt, and finally returned to the rallying-point.

Two other Whippets, A. 356 and A. 350, were detailed to go *via* the cross-roads, round the Triangular Copse, in front of Behagnies and Sapignies. Whilst approaching this point 2/Lieut. W. Millar, whose Whippet had done good work throughout the engagement, was killed, whilst getting out of his Tank, by a shell from an anti-Tank gun, firing from the west end of the village of Sapignies. After that the Whippet itself received a direct hit on the radiator

AYETTE TO HINDENBURG LINE 151

and had to abandon the action, being eventually towed in to the rallying-point. The second Whippet, A. 350, developed mechanical trouble.

The other two Whippets were detailed to work round a sector towards the village of Behagnies. All six Tanks were heavily fired on by machine guns, and were followed by the infantry. At 4.30, the enemy having halted on a line running through Bihucourt towards Behagnies, the Whippets able to do so rallied at Ayette at 6 P.M.

The following Whippets rallied at Ayette:

"A" Company.
   A. 289

"C" Company.
   A. 361
   „ 356 (towed in).
   „ 349
   „ 333
   „ 350
   „ 338
   „ 339

Tanks which did not rally:

"A" Company.

A. 360 Lieut. Muir	.	4 Direct hits.
„ 394 2/Lieut. Pollitt	.	Direct hit.
„ 363 „ Innes	.	„ „
„ 287 Captain J. L. Lees	.	„ „
„ 351 Lieut. Black	.	Engine trouble.

"C" Company.

A. 296 2/Lieut. J. Cummings	.	Direct hit and burnt out.
„ 334 Captain H. N. Morton, M.C.	.	Direct hit and burnt out.

The total casualties for the day were as follows: *Casualties.*

Killed.

Captain J. L. Lees, M.C.
Lieut. J. Black.
2/Lieut. W. Millar.
201148 Private Griffiths, R. N.
201247 ,, Evenden, R. E.

Wounded.

Lieut. A. G. Muir.
2/Lieut. W. H. Pollitt.
,, R. F. Innes.
Captain H. N. Morton, M.C.
2/Lieut. J. V. Cummings.
,, W. J. Murray.
92540 Corporal Scott, L.
Private Bayne.
205323 ,, Bestwick, W. H.
95617 ,, Dolton, P.
,, Gilbert.
201117 Corporal Ingram, A.
95478 Sergeant Fenton, L.
92463 Corporal Holden, J.
69571 Private Budd, P. E.
201155 Sergeant Burchett, J. E.

The next day, August 24, eight Whippets from the Battalion started for action, but on reaching Adinfer were recalled, as the operations were cancelled. Meanwhile, owing to casualties, the following changes had taken place in the command of the Battalion. Lieut.-Col. R. A. West, D.S.O., M.C., became Commanding Officer on the 22/8/18, *vice* Lieut.-Col. R. B. Wood, killed in action 22/8/18. Major J. Leslie, M.C., took command of "A" Company, *vice* Major A. McC. Inglis, D.S.O., wounded in action 8/8/18.

Change in Command.

On August 27 all available Tanks, under

AYETTE TO HINDENBURG LINE 153

Major J. Leslie, M.C., moved to Ayette, whilst B.H.Q. and details remained at Monchy-au-Bois. Next day the Tanks under Major Leslie moved to Gomiecourt.

On August 30 eight Tanks under Major Leslie and Captain J. Munro, M.C., moved to a point about 1000 yards south-east of Mory Copse, but were compelled, about 1 P.M., by heavy shellfire, to move back in front of Ervillers. The projected operations depended on the success of the Mark IV. Tanks, and as these were late in coming up, the Whippets returned to Gomiecourt.

The same evening at 7.30 P.M. five Tanks of Mory Copse. "C" Company, under Captain J. Munro, M.C., and Lieut. E. N. Edwards, M.C., moved up to Mory Copse, and waited there all night. At 4.45 A.M. the Whippets moved up with the object of assisting the infantry to establish themselves at Noreuil Switch and Longatte Trench. Major Leslie arrived at 4.30 A.M. and took charge of the operations.

The action commenced at 5.45 A.M., August 31. Four Tanks under Lieut. Edwards moved forward in echelon formation and cleared up the sector of ground between these two systems. On successfully completing these operations the Tanks returned to Gomiecourt. Action of August 31.

Later in the day it was found that, owing to the fact that the infantry had not followed on, further operations were necessary. Five Tanks, therefore, under the command of Captain J. M. Oke and Lieut. E. N. Edwards, M.C., left Gomiecourt at 7.30 P.M. and reached Mory Copse at 9.15 A.M. Next morning, September 1, they moved from Mory Copse at 4.45. The objective was the same. The Tanks, under Lieut. Edwards, patrolled in echelon formation; no enemy were seen, and the village of Noreuil appeared deserted. The Tanks on coming out of action reported to the 7th and 9th Infantry Brigades, and finally returned to Gomiecourt.

Action of "B" Coy. in front of Corbie.
Whilst the Battalion, consisting of Battalion Headquarters, " A " and " C " Companies, had moved north and joined the VI. Corps, " B " Company, under the command of Major H. Darby, M.C., had remained behind for future operations in front of Corbie.

The trek was made from Le Quesnel to a point south of Morlancourt on August 11. On arriving there the next few days were occupied in cleaning, overhauling, and effecting the necessary repairs.

On August 22 orders were received to assist the Northumberland Fusiliers, III. Corps, on the Bray-Albert Road as far as the citadel. In passing it is interesting to note that this action was fought over the same ground as the Tank Corps Camp, on the Bray-Albert Road, which had been erected by the Corps after the Cambrai battles.

AYETTE TO HINDENBURG LINE 155

The Company moved from their lying-up place at 4.15 A.M., and arrived at the Bois de Tailles at 5.50. Here heavy shelling was encountered from the direction of Le Plateau. The infantry were held up by heavy machine-gun fire from the Bray–Albert Road. Whilst making a reconnaissance in the direction of the old 3rd Brigade Whippet School on the Bray–Albert Road, Major Darby was severely wounded, and had to be evacuated. The command was taken over by Captain W. S. Hopkins, M.C. Towards the evening orders were received to return to Cemetery Copse, which was reached about 3 P.M.

Later in the day two Whippets, under Lieut. A. L. Watkins, M.C., were ordered to join the 37th Infantry Brigade, and stand by in order to break up counter-attacks. They were, however, not needed, and joined the remainder of the Company, at Cemetery Copse, about 3 A.M. on the morning of August 23.

On the 24th of August three Whippets, under Captain C. H. Strachan, left Cemetery Copse at 9 A.M. and proceeded to the Bray–Albert Road. At 1.30 P.M. they advanced with the 37th Infantry Brigade towards Happy Valley. Here they encountered very heavy machine-gun and trench-mortar fire. The infantry made some headway. Captain Strachan's Tank received a direct hit. As the Tanks were unable to render any further assistance they withdrew to Cemetery Copse at 3 P.M.

<small>"B" Coy. rejoins Battalion.</small> On August 31 the Company entrained at Mericourt l'Abbé, and proceeded to Boisleaux-au-Mont, trekking from there to Gomiecourt, rejoining " A " and " C " Companies at the new camp east of the village, B.H.Q. having moved up the same day. The whole Battalion were assembled under the command of Lieut.-Col. R. A. West, D.S.O., M.C.

<small>Attack near Vaulx-Vraucourt.</small> On September 1 two Tanks under 2/Lieuts. F. Mosley and Avin, in conjunction with the 62nd Division, made an attack on a strong point in front of Vaulx-Vraucourt. These Tanks were met with intense machine-gun fire, and for a time had to turn back, but eventually got the infantry on to their objectives. The Tank commanded by Lieut. Mosley was pierced by A.P. bullets; whilst destroying a machine-gun position by crushing it became ditched, the Tank catching fire. The crew were all wounded. A fine piece of rescue work was effected by Private W. Sidell, who brought the driver (Private Tacchi) back a considerable distance under fire.

The following casualties occurred during the day :

Wounded.
2/Lieut. H. E. Avin.
,, F. F. Mosley.
93011 Private Brown, F. A.
305933 Corporal Shooter, W.
307601 Private Tacchi, W.

On the night September 1-2, nine Whippets, under Captain C. H. Strachan, left Gomiecourt to attack in the direction of Lagnicourt. Owing to the pressure at which the Tanks had been working for the last five weeks, little time had been available for overhauling, and as the Tanks were running badly it was impossible to get them up in time for the operations. The Commanding Officer, Lieut.-Col. R. A. West, D.S.O., M.C., left camp early on the morning of September 2 with two mounted orderlies. It was his intention to get up with the Whippets before they went into action, by Lagnicourt. He went as far as the infantry on horseback in order to watch the progress of the battle and to ascertain when to send the Whippets forward. He arrived at the front line when the enemy were in progress of delivering a strong local counter-attack. The Infantry Battalion had suffered heavy officer casualties and its flanks were exposed. Realising that there was a danger of the Battalion giving way, he at once rode in front of them, under extremely heavy machine-gun and rifle fire, and rallied the men. In spite of the fact that the enemy were close up on him, he took charge of the situation and detailed N.C.O.'s to replace officer casualties. He then rode up and down in front of the men, in face of certain death, encouraging all, and calling upon them to "Stick it, men, and show them fight."

Lagnicourt.

Death of Lt.-Col. R. A. West, D.S.O., M.C.

His last words were, "For God's sake, put up a good fight." For this heroic self-sacrifice Colonel West was awarded the Victoria Cross. When Lieut.-Col. West came to the Battalion as O.C. "C" Company, he had been awarded the D.S.O. for splendid work in the Arras battles. Whilst with the Battalion, within the short space of time between August 8 and September 2, he was awarded the V.C., Bar to D.S.O., and the M.C.

On the death of Lieut.-Colonel R. A. West, V.C., D.S.O., M.C., Major W. O. Gibbs assumed command of the Battalion, and at once saw the G.O.C. 8th Infantry Brigade, who asked for two Whippets to go and clear up the enemy machine guns in the trenches north of the Bois de Vaulx. By this time it was possible to get two Whippets going, and these under Captain Oke, Sergeant Squires and Corporal Cossum being in charge of the Tanks, proceeded to a point just west of St. Leger, Vraucourt Road. With two Companies of the Suffolk Regiment the Whippets should go forward and consolidate the line of the ridge, over which the road from Noreuil to Lagnicourt passed. The operation only lasted half an hour. It was completely successful, and resulted in driving between 50 and 60 prisoners back on to the infantry.

The following casualties occurred during the day :

Wounded.
69638 Corporal Cossum, F. H.
69572 Lance-Corporal Hellier, F. C.
92592 Private Byrne, M.

At 4 P.M. on the 2nd orders came to hand to place six Whippets, under the command of Major J. Leslie, M.C., in 6th Corps Reserve, ready to exploit a success, should opportunity arise, as a result of an attack by the 6th and 99th Infantry Brigades.

On the 3rd at 9 A.M. orders were received by the detachment to get into touch with the G.O.C. 2nd Division at Vaulx-Vraucourt, at 10.15. It had been ascertained that the enemy had evacuated this line during the night, and the Whippets were required to get into touch with him and co-operate with the 6th Infantry Brigade, whose headquarters were at Maricourt Wood, and seize the high ground between Demicourt and Hermies. The Whippets with a squadron of Q.O.O.H. were to push forward and make good Demicourt and Hermies for the infantry. At 2.20 P.M. Major Leslie was able to send back a message to the effect that the Whippets were on the line Demicourt–Hermies; and that there were no signs of the enemy, but that the enemy was shelling Boursies. *Withdrawal of enemy.*

At 2.45 the enemy guns opened fire on Hermies, and the Whippets went forward towards the Canal, and although in full view of the *Hermies.*

enemy, were not fired upon. They patrolled as far as the old trench system, which was too wide for them to cross, so they thereupon returned to Hermies, where they gave assistance to the infantry in clearing the sunken roads in the vicinity. Two Tanks had to be abandoned on the trench system. They developed bad mechanical trouble, and repairs could not be effected. The remaining four Whippets returned to Gomiecourt, where the Battalion spent the next few days.

After the actions of the Whippets towards Hermies, all remaining Tanks and personnel concentrated at Gomiecourt, accommodation being found for the Battalion in the old Nissen Huts, east of the village, on the Ervillers Road. Tents were erected for the accommodation of officers. These huts were in a very bad condition, having survived the actions during the previous months, so that several days' work was necessary in order to render them partially water-tight and habitable.

Change in command. Lieut.-Colonel Lord Somers, M.C., assumed command of the Battalion on the 8th, taking over from Major Gibbs, Major H. Lane, M.C., being transferred from a Company in the 9th Tank Battalion, and posted as second in command to Colonel Lord Somers.

Work on Tanks was carried on under Company arrangements, and a training programme drawn up for Company courses to commence.

T/LT.-COL. LORD SOMERS, D.S.O., M.C.

AYETTE TO HINDENBURG LINE 161

Instructions were received on the 8th that the Battalion would move on or about the 12th to Saulty area, as soon as suitable billets could be found. Minor repairs were then hurried on, as several Whippets were still unfit for a long trek.

A billeting party searched the St. Amand–Humber Camp area for billets, finally finding sufficient accommodation in Saulty, as the whole area was under close billeting, many infantry units having returned to their training areas.

On the morning of the 12th, twenty-three Whippets commenced the trek at 7 A.M. to Saulty. Owing to the heavy going, due to recent rain, speed was rather below normal, five hours being taken for the journey, a distance of approximately fourteen miles. All Tanks arrived at Saulty about noon, without trouble or incident, the routes and districts being well known to the majority of the crews. Tanks parked up at Saulty in an orchard and field previously selected.

Move to Saulty.

Headquarters' personnel, equipment officer's stores, etc., moved from Gomiecourt by lorry. Saulty Château, being at the moment unoccupied, was allotted to the Battalion, Headquarters being disposed there. " C " Company mess, unable to find a suitable room, took over the remainder of the accommodation. Companies were billeted in the village, in barns.

The next two days passed without incident, crews working on Tanks, correcting faults brought

M

to light by trekking, spare men repairing billets and performing necessary camp duties.

A few lorries now being available for use, it was decided to partially clear the old dump at Bois de Naours, where much necessary heavy stores and material had been left. This was effected, essential material being brought and distributed again to Companies.

At this period the inevitable rumour of a further move again became popular. In this case it was more accurate than usual, as preliminary orders were received, on the day following, of a possible move to the Lucheux area, the trouble being shortage of accommodation for a Battalion.

The commanding officer visited 3rd Brigade Headquarters at Bouquemaison, and arrangements were made for an allotment of billets for the Battalion at Neuvillette.

Move to Neuvillette.
On the 17th, twenty-three Tanks left Saulty about 9 A.M. and commenced trekking to Neuvillette, a cross-country route being chosen as much as possible, distance being approximately twelve miles. Good time was made on the trek, all Whippets arriving at this village shortly after noon.

Good billets were found for Headquarters, and two Companies, "A" and "C," in Neuvillette, but owing to many of the barns being full of the season's crop of corn, and others in use,

AYETTE TO HINDENBURG LINE 163

the full accommodation could not be secured. O.C. " B " Company therefore decided to trek an additional two kilos and dispose the Company at Canteleux, a small village to the north of Neuvillette, where ample accommodation existed for a detached Company. Whippets therefore trekked to Canteleux during the afternoon and parked up.

The following day was spent in Company re-organisation, work on defective Tanks, cleaning up, and repairing billets.

The following honours and awards were granted for these actions : _{Honours and Awards.}

Victoria Cross.
Lieut.-Colonel R. A. West, D.S.O., M.C.

Bar to Distinguished Service Order.
Lieut.-Colonel R. A. West, D.S.O., M.C.

Distinguished Service Order.
Major J. Leslie, M.C.

Bar to Military Cross.
Captain T. K. Robson, M.C.

Military Cross.
Captain A. R. Chapman.
2/Lieut. F. F. Bromley.
„ E. N. Edwards.
„ H. A. Avins.

Distinguished Conduct Medal.
77365 Corporal Prest, W.
93000 Private Sidell, W.
92995 „ Bussey, B. F.

Military Medal.

309077 Lance-Corporal Balls, T. H.
69537 Private Peterson, M.
69638 Corporal Cossum, F.
93011 Private Brown, F. A.
93009 ,, Stannard, H. V.
305933 Corporal Shooter, W. H.

CHAPTER XI

FROM TINCOURT TO ELINCOURT

ON September 19, preliminary movement orders were received from Headquarters, 3rd Brigade, for the Battalion to be prepared to entrain at Bouquemaison on or about the 23rd, probable destination being the Peronne area. The ramp and station approaches were examined at Bouquemaison, and necessary arrangements made with the R.T.O. Work on Tanks was pushed forward with all speed, there being several temporarily unfit awaiting the arrival of spares. *[Preparations for move to Peronne Area.]*

On the day following, a Brigade Conference was convened by Brigadier-General Hardress Lloyd, D.S.O., at the Brigade Headquarters, Bouquemaison. Details of the forthcoming operations were explained and discussed, and preliminary arrangements agreed upon.

The Battalion was to entrain at Bouquemaison on the 22nd, proceed by rail to Tincourt, four miles east of Peronne, and park up north of the railway, Tincourt being then the railhead for the Peronne area.

On the 21st, all necessary arrangements were made by O.C. Companies for entrainment on the morrow. Maps and details of the new area were received from Brigade and re-distributed to Companies for information.

<small>Move to Tincourt.</small> Ten Whippets of "C" Company and six Whippets of "A" Company trekked to Bouquemaison Station during the morning, a distance of approximately $1\frac{1}{2}$ miles, parking up in the station yard awaiting the arrival of the train. This arrived to schedule, and Tanks were entrained without difficulty, leaving at 2.30 P.M.

Meanwhile an advance party had proceeded to Tincourt by road, where a temporary camp site was selected at Bois de Buire, with Tank park adjoining. A few tents were erected by this party, and arrangements made to meet the train and guide the Tanks up. The first train from Bouquemaison arrived at Tincourt at 1 A.M. on the 23rd. Little difficulty was met with in detraining, despite the use of a side ramp in lieu of the usual end-on type. Tanks were trekked to Bois de Buire, one mile north of Tincourt, and parked in the Wood.

The second train, consisting of the remaining Whippets, four "A" Company, together with eleven of "B" Company and one of "C" Company, left Bouquemaison during the afternoon of the 23rd. Two Whippets were left at Neuvillette, one of "A" Company and the other

"B" Company, being unfit for trekking owing to lack of spares.

All Battalion and Company heavy stores were left behind at a Battalion dump in Neuvillette under a guard.

On the 23rd, stores brought up on the first train to Tincourt were lorried during the morning to the camp site at Bois de Buire. During the afternoon a wire was received from 3rd Brigade to the effect that Tanks were to concentrate to the south of the railway, and not on the north side as previously instructed. A small copse about 2000 yards south of Tincourt was therefore chosen as a camp site and Tank park, and all arrangements made to erect temporary shelters, and to meet and guide the Whippets up.

The second Tank train from Bouquemaison arrived at Tincourt about 5.30 P.M., the Tanks being quickly detrained and trekked cross country to the camp and Tank park. Stores from the train were lorried up from the station, and a few tents erected. Owing to the congestion of traffic, due to the heavy concentration of all arms in the area, and other Tanks also arriving at Tincourt, it was deemed advisable to leave the Tanks, then at Bois de Buire, for a further twenty-four hours, and trek them to the copse, south of the railway, on the day following.

On the 24th the temporary camp was much improved upon during the day, Company lines being established and small cook-houses being built. Crews also worked on maintenance on several defective Tanks.

Excellent camouflage existed at the copse, Tanks being lined up on the southern and eastern edges, consequently crews were able to work on their buses under natural cover.

During the afternoon the Whippets from the second Tank train trekked from Bois de Buire, through Tincourt, to the new camp. No difficulties were met with *en route,* the day being without incident.

Reconnaissance for Forward Area.

Reconnaissance officers and section commanders commenced a general study and examination of the ground eastwards towards Hargicourt, Villeret, and Le Verguier, this area being indicated as a possible sector for the Battalion in the anticipated operations. 3rd Tank Brigade was now being held in Army Reserve.

From the 25th to the 29th was a period of preparation and study of the ground in an easterly direction. Work on Tanks was pushed forward, and all were soon fit for action. Routes, lying-up points, dump sites, refilling points, railway crossings, etc., were all examined, arrangements being made jointly with 9th Tank Battalion, as many portions of the route overlapped and could be used mutually. A suitable

FROM TINCOURT TO ELINCOURT

lying-up point was selected in the valley west of Grand Priol Woods, and routes from this point eastwards, towards the St. Quentin Canal, examined and checked. 3rd Tank Brigade was allotted this day to the IX. Corps from Army Reserve.

On the 26th of September, 3rd Tank Brigade consisted of 5th, 6th, and 9th Tank Battalions. Allotments to Infantry Divisions were made as follows : *Allotments of Battalions to Divisions of IX. Corps.*

> Two Companies of 9th Battalion to 46th Division.
>
> One Company 6th Battalion, and one Company 9th Battalion to 32nd Division, for operations against the Hindenburg Defences between St. Quentin and Vendhuile.
>
> 5th Battalion and two Companies 6th Battalion held in Corps Reserve.

Distinguishing signs were now painted on all Whippets, IX. Corps sign being a large red IX., the 32nd Division sign being ⁑ in white.

Instructions received later stated that one Company of the Battalion was to operate with the 97th Infantry Brigade, and all Tanks to cross the St. Quentin Canal as close to the southern entrance of the Bellicourt Tunnel as possible.

Liaison was at once established with the 97th Infantry Brigade and the 32nd Division, Headquarters Battalion commanders arranging details of the attack direct with the G.O.C. Division.

Move forward of "A" Company.

On the 27th, one Company of nine Tanks, under Captain R. E. Howell, O.C. " A " Company, moved at 7 P.M. on route previously arranged, to lying-up point one mile north of Le Verguier and approximately three miles east of the Canal at Bellicourt, the Roisel–Montigny railway being crossed at a prepared ramped crossing in order to avoid damage.

" B " and " C " Companies were in Corps Reserve at the copse south of Tincourt. Communication was maintained with the G.O.C. 97th Infantry Brigade.

General Instructions for September 29.

On the 28th, Y-Z day, the following orders and general instructions were issued to officers commanding Companies :

" A " Company to move from their lying-up point on orders from the Commanding Officer, to pick up the infantry of the 97th Brigade.

" B " and " C " Companies to operate with the 96th Infantry Brigade, and to move on morning of Z day from present position at Tincourt to lying-up point now occupied by " A " Company, thus keeping in close reserve to " A " Company.

Officers from " A " Company went forward and examined their route from lying-up points towards the Canal, crossing at Bellicourt.

On the 29th, Z day, Battalion Headquarters established at dawn at the 32nd Divisional Advanced Headquarters, at Canbrières Woods, one mile south of Le Verguier, a line being granted on the Divisional switchboard, and an

FROM TINCOURT TO ELINCOURT

Aeroplane Dropping Station established. Owing to the heavy mist on the morning no messages were received by aeroplane until 11 A.M.

Tanks of "B" and "C" Companies left Tincourt at dawn, arriving at lying-up point about 10 A.M.; the route previously used by "A" Company was followed, and no difficulties were met with. <small>Move of "B" and "C" Companies.</small>

On receipt of orders, Tanks moved off from the lying-up point at 11.45, arriving at Magny-la-Fosse at 2 P.M., and here got in touch with the 32nd Division. An attack was organised with the object of securing the Lehaucourt Ridge, and at 4.45 four Tanks, under Lieut. V. G. Sanders, moved forward with the Border Regiment. The attack was entirely successful, and the Tanks returned at 5.25 P.M.

A report came through that there was a gap in our line south of the village of Joncourt, and two Tanks, with a Company of Argylls, left at 6 P.M. to close up this gap. At the same time four Tanks were sent up the valley to Lehaucourt Ridge to clear up some troublesome machine-gun posts. The latter patrolled for some time in front of the infantry, silencing the machine guns, and returned to the rallying-point at 8.15 P.M. The two Tanks working with the Argylls were successful in helping to close up the gap in the line, but as they were about to rally a shell burst between the tracks of A. 389, and the Tank <small>Action of "A" Company.</small>

172 THE SIXTH TANK BATTALION

could not be moved. Finally, eight Tanks rallied south of Magny-la-Fosse at 8.30 P.M.

A Brigade rallying-point was established at Springbok Valley, 1000 yards west of Magny-la-Fosse and 500 yards east of the Canal.

Tanks of " B " and " C " Companies were moved eastwards towards the canal about one mile, lying up in the valley near Chakan–Grand Priol Woods for the night.

On the 30th, orders were received from the 3rd Brigade to the effect : 32nd Division was to attack the Beaurevoir–Masnières Line on the 1st of October. O.C. 6th Battalion to arrange details with G.O.C. 32nd Division, and be prepared to employ Whippets should a suitable opportunity occur.

Action of " A " Company on September 30.
Tanks of " A " Company, under Captain R. E. Howell, co-operated with the 14th Infantry Brigade in the attack on Joncourt.

At 12.30 P.M. on the 30th, O.C. " A " Company effected liaison with the G.O.C. 14th Infantry Brigade, with a view to attacking Joncourt in conjunction with the 15th Lancashire Fusiliers. It was arranged for three Tanks to move to a point 800 yards north-east of Magny-la-Fosse, and from there proceed up the valley towards Joncourt, entering the village from the south, and assisting the infantry, who were lying up west and south of the village. At 2.30 P.M. three Tanks, under Captain J. J. Farrar, M.C., moved off to the point north-east of Magny, arriving there at 2.45 P.M. One Tank was left here in reserve, and the other two moved off to the attack at 3.30 P.M. On approaching the railway south of Joncourt they came under heavy machine-gun and anti-Tank fire. Lieut. Holloway's Tank received three hits from an anti-Tank gun and was put out of action. The second tank reached the outskirts of the village, but, as no infantry followed, returned to try and pick them up. Failing, however, to get in touch with the infantry, and with engines running badly, it returned to the valley. The reserve Tank was then sent up to work right through the village, but was knocked out by anti-Tank fire just south of the railway at Joncourt.

The following casualties occurred on this date :

Wounded.
2/Lieut. J. A. Holloway.
92344 Private Bayne, A.

Tanks of " B " and " C " Companies, under orders from the commanding officer, moved forward from the Grand Priol Woods at 3 P.M. to the rallying-point at Springbok Valley, arriving without trouble, having followed " A " Company's tracks and crossing the Canal south of Bellicourt. All Tanks of this Battalion were now concentrated at the Brigade rallying-point at Springbok Valley.

On October 1, orders were received early in the day from the G.O.C. 32nd Division that the

Division would attempt to break through the Beaurevoir–Fonsomme Line during the afternoon. "C" Company's Tanks were then removed from the Brigade rallying-point at Springbok Valley to Fosse Wood, to comply with orders received, but were not used for this action, their assistance being unnecessary. These Tanks were lying up south of Joncourt during the 2nd and 3rd, in conjunction with the 1st Squadron 20th Hussars. The situation being too indefinite for their use in conjunction with the cavalry screen, it was finally decided to withdraw them to the Brigade rallying-point at Springbok Valley.

The next few days were spent in overhauling defective Tanks; "A" Company trekking back to Le Verguier, and held in reserve. Battalion Headquarters were already established in the copse east of the village.

Orders were received, on the 6th, of an impending action on the 8th. Whippets were to assist in the capture of the red dotted line east of Brancourt, and to exploit the area north-eastwards towards Premont.

"A" Company, consisting of two sections, each of three Whippets, were to operate on the extreme right with the 6th Division. One section was to assist the infantry on to the red line, and then another section was to exploit the area immediately in front of Fresnoy-le-Grand.

FROM TINCOURT TO ELINCOURT 175

The officer commanding "A" Company interviewed all the Brigade commanders with whom his Company was to operate, on the 7th of October.

All the Tank commanders and section commanders went over the ground on the 7th, examining all possible routes and getting a view of the ground over which they were to operate, in the direction of Fresnoy-le-Grand, from an observation post near Preselles. A difficult portion of the route was taped on the evening of the 7th.

The same evening the six Whippets of "A" Company left camp and moved to their lying-up point at Fosse Wood.

On the morning of the 8th, one section of three Whippets, under Lieut. V. G. Sanders, moved forward behind the infantry at 4.50 A.M. and got into action at 7.50 A.M. They found the infantry slightly held up about 1000 yards south of Brancourt. They then proceeded to the Sunken Road, where the enemy were holding out, and engaged him at close range, 15 to 20 yards dividing him in the direction of Fresnoy. *Action on October 8.*

Lieut. V. G. Sanders turned his Whippet in the direction of Brancourt, and obtained good targets as the enemy left the village. All three Whippets experienced heavy fire from machine guns using A.P. bullets. No. 331, owing to a broken fan chain, had to return to the fork roads east of Montbrehain, where it completely broke down. The other two Tanks continued in the area of exploitation until 8.45 A.M., when they became immobile to the east of Brancourt. Both officers were wounded; 2/Lieut. G. Reed got back to our lines, and reported 2/Lieut. P. Jones badly hit and his crew prisoners.

The right section, under Lieut. W. Underhill, left the starting-point at zero, and crossing our line at 5.30 A.M. came under heavy machine-gun fire and shell fire. As the infantry were not following, they returned and helped them forward. No. 351 had a loophole plate blown off, and the officer became a casualty. As the attack could not proceed, the Whippet was brought into the rallying-point at 11 A.M. After proceeding into action, A. 261 had the high tension leads cut by an A.P. bullet, and had to be left at a point north of Sequehart; the officer was a casualty. No. 378, after repairing a broken fan chain, was able to return at slow speed to the rallying-point.

The following Tanks rallied at the rallying-point:

A. 351, A. 378, A. 331.

The following Tanks were rendered immobile by A.P. bullets, and remained to the east of Brancourt:

A. 228, A. 381.

The armament of a Whippet is not strong enough for assisting in an infantry attack on definite objectives when a flank is exposed. In this action, owing to the French attack not progressing, the heavy enemy machine guns were able to concentrate on the Whippets operating in the valley. This meant that the Whippet had to deal with heavy armour-piercing machine guns' fire from the front and flank. The crew is not large enough to deal with concentrated heavy machine guns successfully. One Mark V. male Tank could have dealt successfully with the flank guns, whilst the Whippets were dealing with the opposition in front.

" B " and " C " Companies were detailed to work on the left, in the direction of Premont, with the American Division. The Company commanders got in touch with the commanding officers of the infantry units.

" B " Company were to operate with the 118th American Regiment, and " C " Company with the 117th American Regiment.

The reconnaissance officers and all section commanders examined the front line up to Montbrehain.

The Companies moved forward from the lying-up place, behind Joncourt, at 5.15 A.M., this time being calculated to bring them on the Red Line by zero plus 3.10 hours.

The ground in the enemy territory was

surveyed by the officers from the observation post behind Ramicourt.

"B" Company operated on the right with six Whippets. Tank A. 377 had developed mechanical trouble, and did not start, but five Tanks, A. 332, A. 330, A. 369, A. 347, and A. 370, were launched at zero plus 165 minutes. Captain Strachan's section led, followed by Captain Allen's section. They reached the dotted red line between zero plus 169 minutes and zero plus 174 minutes, and proceeded towards their various objectives, in diamond formation.

The Company commander took up his position on the ridge to the left of Brancourt, and observed Captain Allen's section going well ahead, but apparently unsupported, except for a few isolated groups of infantry. The enemy put down a very heavy barrage on the northwest edge of Brancourt.

Tank A. 377 reported about this time, and was sent after Captain Strachan's section. It was about five minutes behind them.

The left flank met heavy opposition about 7.45 A.M. in the neighbourhood of Vaux-le-Pretre. One Tank was set on fire in front of Fraicourt Wood, and another, A. 330, shortly after.

About 10.15 A.M. Captain Strachan's section rallied north of Montbrehain. Captain Allen's Tank had received a direct hit, but proceeded

FROM TINCOURT TO ELINCOURT 179

towards the rallying-point. The infantry appeared to have gained their objectives; Captain Strachan's section therefore proceeded to the rallying-point.

All Tanks came into contact with the enemy, and about 3000 rounds S.A.A. were expended.

"C" Company, consisting of ten Whippets, had as their objective the far side of Premont.

No. 9 section, under 2/Lieut. F. F. Bromley, M.C., and No. 10 section, under Captain J. Munro, M.C., with three Whippets each, started at 6.45 A.M., picking up their infantry on the Red Line, and proceeded in diamond formation towards their objective, Captain Munro's section taking the right, and Lieut. Bromley's section the left, with the idea of making a demonstration in front of the village, to enable the infantry to gain a footing, then to encircle the place to prevent the enemy retiring.

The remaining four Whippets started at 7.0 A.M., under Lieut. T. G. L. Taylor, proceeding in rear of the other two sections. At about 7.30 A.M. Lieut. Taylor became a casualty, and his Tank was sent on to Captain Munro, M.C., the other three joining Lieut. Bromley, M.C.

Captain Munro, M.C., reached Vaux-le-Pretre with two Whippets, and he reported that the infantry were on their objective on the left of the village. He was then ordered to return to the rallying-point. His third Whippet (Sergeant

Squires), No. 338, had received a direct hit and was burnt out, the crew all being killed.

Two of the remaining Whippets had mechanical trouble—one was unable to proceed past the Red Line, but the other (Corporal Reed) joined Lieut. Bromley's section, after the crew had worked hard, under heavy shell fire, to rectify the trouble.

Lieut. Bromley, M.C., got in touch with the infantry about 7.55 A.M. on the north edge of Vaux-le-Pretre, when the remaining Whippets of the reserve section arrived. He met the infantry commander, and arranged to proceed up the Beaver Dell Valley, the infantry following behind. Good targets were obtained, and the Whippets rallied at Joncourt, and when the infantry arrived, went forward to escort them through the village of Premont. The Whippets were not fired upon from the village, and the infantry then occupied it, the Tanks rallying north of Vaux-le-Pretre.

All Tanks, with the exception of 338 (Sergeant Squires) rallied at the Company rallying-point at Joncourt.

All Tanks came into contact with the enemy, and an estimated quantity of 6500 rounds of S.A.A. was expended.

"B" Company's Tanks rallied at Joncourt as follows :

A. 347, A. 379, A. 332, A. 377, A. 313.

The following Whippets received direct hits and were burnt out:

    A. 369 (N.E. of Brancourt).
    A. 330   ,,   ,,

"C" Company's Tanks rallied as follows:

A. 333, A. 350, A. 361, A. 368, A. 349, A. 321, A. 358, A. 328, A. 339.

A. 338 received a direct hit and was burnt out at Brancourt.

It appears from this action of "B" and "C" Companies that the correct formation for Whippets is depth. Being in diamond formation, with the leading Tank well ahead, enabled the remaining Tanks of Captain Munro's section to avoid the anti-Tank gun which hit No. 338, and by another approach to put the crew of the gun out of action. Similarly, against the two batteries which were in position north of Vaux-le-Pretre, the leading Whippet was able to locate the batteries, and the remaining Whippets were then able to take them in the flank from the south. Sections worked in echelon, the northern, or left flank, thrown forward. <small>Lessons learned from this Battle.</small>

In attacking small localities, an intermittent fire directed on them was successful in keeping enemy anti-Tank and machine guns quiet, until the Whippets were right on top of them. Fraicourt Wood, however, was too large for this kind of fire to be effective, consequently the two

182 THE SIXTH TANK BATTALION

Tanks of " B " Company were hit from the wood. Co-operation by our own machine guns, or Lewis guns, on a locality of this kind would be invaluable, and enable Whippets to approach close enough to discover emplacements. This kind of fire could easily have been directed in this case from the Red Line, and provided A.P. ammunition was not used, Whippets could have gone close up to the wood without danger.

Casualties. The following are the total casualties in these actions of " A," " B " and " C " Companies :

Killed.
69521 Sergeant Squires, J. G.
306120 Private Wilson, A. G.
91766   ,,   Godley, R.
111758   ,,   Davies, A.
309107   ,,   Pamphilon, J. A.

Wounded.
Captain J. Allen, M.C.
Lieut. T. G. L. Taylor.
2/Lieut. G. Reed.
  ,,   A. M'Allister.
  ,,   R. R. Turner.
Lieut. C. Underhill.
2/Lieut. P. P. Jones. (Died of Wounds.)
308429 Private Quinn, F. G.
201136   ,,   Lake, R. E.
92481   ,,   Hamer, L.
69720 Corporal Howlett, G. F.
306252 Private Richardson, E. H.

Missing.
92526 Lance-Corporal Cargill, G. T.
111683 Private Turnbull, A. E.
305217   ,,   Kennedy, J.
94970   ,,   Drake, A. E. J.

FROM TINCOURT TO ELINCOURT 183

After these operations Companies were concentrated at Elincourt, Battalion Headquarters also being established there on the 11th, Tanks trekking from their rallying-point on the day following. 4th Brigade Headquarters were established at Serain. Billets were provided in the village for the Battalion, there being ample accommodation, as few civilians had been allowed to remain by the retreating enemy. *Elincourt.*

A selected number of N.C.O.'s and other ranks, to complete the establishment of the new Battalions in England, left the Battalion on the 12th, and proceeded to the rear headquarters at Neuvillette, to await sailing orders. The party was struck off the strength on the 17th. *Departure of Personnel for new Battalions.*

Work was at once commenced on defective Tanks, and Companies generally reorganised for further operations.

A conference at 4th Brigade Headquarters at Serain was convened on the 13th, and preliminary orders issued for an attack by the 1st Division on the 17th, with whom Whippets were to co-operate. *Conference at 4th Tank Brigade Headquarters.*

Orders were received from 4th Tank Brigade on the 13th, that the Fourth Army would resume the offensive between Andigny-les-Firmes and Montay on or about the 17th inst. The Battalion consisting of sixteen Whippets was allotted to the IX. Corps. *Preparations for Battle of Selle River, October 17.*

"B" Company received orders on the 15th

that four Tanks would be required to co-operate with the 2nd K.R.R.C., with whom they were to assist either to capture the Green Line, if sufficient Heavy Tanks were not available after the capture of the Red Line, or to follow up the Battle in Reserve to the Company commanded by Major W. O. Gibbs, in the event of not being employed during the advance to the Green Line.

"C" Company were attached to the 1st Division, for employment in exploitation beyond the Green Line, in the direction towards the canal and south of Revet-de-Beaulieu. A composite Company was formed, consisting of eight Tanks of "C" Company, and two "B" Company, and two "A" Company.

The Company commanders visited Divisional and Brigade Headquarters on the 14th, 15th and 16th, and personally saw officers commanding infantry units they were working with. All Company officers met the Commanding Officer and officers of the infantry with whom they were operating.

During the 14th and 15th, reconnaissance officers and Company officers examined the ground from Elincourt towards centre of IX. Corps back area. Lying-up points were noted, crossings over Busigny–Bohain railway examined, and the general route from Elincourt to above points carefully checked. A chart of air lines and cables was obtained from the XIII. Corps,

FROM TINCOURT TO ELINCOURT

and routes arranged to avoid any points where damage would be caused by Tanks. Company commanders, reconnaissance officers, and all Tank commanders also walked over the ground east of Busigny–Bohain Road, and examined forward areas from high ground on the right of Mont d'Origny. Tank commanders also layered their maps.

Photographs were received on Y day; these were examined by all officers and drivers, and proved extremely useful.

The River Selle, south of Molain, appeared to be no obstacle, and in view of this the O.C. " B " Company decided to cross at a level crossing south of Molain, and work north of the railway exclusively.

Five Tanks of " B " Company, and twelve Tanks of the composite Company moved on the afternoon of the 16th, to a lying-up point in La Sablière Bois just off the Bohain–Busigny Road.

Communications were effected by dismounted orderlies. B.H.Q. was established to the west of Vaux-Andigny, and Company Headquarters close to the railway-crossing south of Molain, and Advanced Headquarters " B " Company were established with the 2nd K.R.R.C. south-west of Molain, and were withdrawn to the quarry by the railway-crossing south of Molain when Tanks rallied after these operations.

The Company rallying-point was established at the quarry by the railway-crossing, and the Battalion rallying-point north of Vaux-Andigny.

The Battalion dump was formed at a point on the Bohain–Busigny Road close to where the Tanks were lying up on the 16th.

Action on October 17. At 10 A.M. the infantry were badly held up by machine guns, and apparently unsupported on their flanks at a point about 2000 yards to the west of Molain. Officer commanding " B " Company therefore sent 2/Lieut. G. F. Smith to get the Tanks up to this position, intending to employ them in whatever way the situation demanded. Four Tanks arrived shortly after 11 A.M., A. 335, A. 379, A. 321, and A. 347, and were ordered to assist the infantry to capture the Red Line as follows :

A. 321. To clear up the machine guns in the copses north of La Vallée Mulâtre, etc.
A. 379. To work round Demilieu from the north.
A. 377. To work round Demilieu from the south.
A. 347. To work round Demilieu from the south-east.

A. 321 patrolled the ground as directed, and silenced several machine guns, but the infantry were unable to advance.

A. 379, A. 377, and A. 347 all converged on Demilieu, but were all knocked out in turn by a field gun, situated either in Demilieu or Bellevue. The machine-gun fire was extremely heavy, and the infantry were only able to advance with

FROM TINCOURT TO ELINCOURT 187

difficulty behind the Tanks. When the latter were put out of action the infantry were forced to withdraw about 200 yards.

Tank A. 321 returned to the rallying-point, situated in the quarry, at 1.30 P.M., and then the Company commander remained there with the Tanks until 4 P.M., when the O.C. 2nd K.R.R.C. informed him tha he could be of no further assistance to him. The Tank was, therefore, taken back to the Battalion rallying-point north of Vaux-Andigny.

At 7.15 hours on Z day " C " Company (twelve Tanks) moved to the parking-up point in La Sablière Bois just off the Bohain–Busigny Road, and a halt was made near the wood north of Bohain for about an hour, as no definite news had been received. At 10 A.M. Tanks proceeded to the quarry (Company rallying-point), remaining there for further orders.

At 12.30 P.M. one section of Tanks was sent forward in support to " B " Company. At about 1 P.M. Major W. O. Gibbs, O.C. Composite Company, went forward from the quarry to obtain information of the four Tanks, and became a casualty. 2/Lieut. Lloyd took over command of the Composite Company. At 4 P.M. news was received that the four Tanks sent up in support to " B " Company would not be required. They were accordingly withdrawn to the Company rallying-point in the quarry. The

188 THE SIXTH TANK BATTALION

Composite Company then returned to the Battalion rallying-point, north of Vaux-Andigny, at 5.20 P.M. The Company was then held in reserve to operate with the 3rd Infantry Brigade, on Z plus 1 day, if required. Liaison was established and held with the 3rd Infantry Brigade by a runner. These Tanks were not required, and they received orders at 4.30 A.M. (Z plus 1 day) to return to Elincourt. Tanks returned *via* the route chosen south of La Sablière Bois, arriving at Elincourt without difficulty about 12 midnight.

Casualties. The following casualties occurred during this action :

Killed.
78683 Private White, R. A.
201143   ,,   Preston, J. H.
92634 Corporal Stones, H. S.

Wounded.
Major W. O. Gibbs.
 92657 Private Stephens, D.
201220   ,,   Gill, A. E.
305778   ,,   Cross, T. J.
201168   ,,   Smith, P.
 92481   ,,   Hamer, W. L.
201180 Corporal Williams, H. G. L.
 93001 Corporal Brown, F. L.
 94912 Private Cantrell, F.

The following Whippets rallied at La Sablière Bois :

A. 335, A. 321, A. 361, A. 358, A. 333, A. 244, A. 328 A. 339, A. 350, A. 376.

The following received direct hits:

A. 379, A. 377, A. 347.

Fourteen Tanks returned to the Tankodrome at Elincourt on October 18.

2nd Tank Brigade took over the Battalion from the 4th Tank Brigade on the 19th. The Battalion was withdrawn, and training programmes drawn up for Company instruction. *Transfer to 2nd Tank Brigade.*

The Tanks of the 2nd Brigade co-operated in an attack on the 23rd, north of Le Cateau, towards Bois L'Évêque and Bois de Mormal. This Battalion did not operate on this occasion.

Companies were splendidly situated at Elincourt, and proceeded to fully reorganise, check equipment, guns, etc., and to carry out tactical exercises, for section and Company training. An excellent training and exercise ground for Whippets existed in the north of the village; advantage was taken of this to train the crews in various tactical formations in use when co-operating with the infantry. *Training at Elincourt.*

New Company cook-houses were erected or repaired, and baths instituted, and everything possible done to make the personnel fit and healthy. The XIII. Corps concert party gave excellent performances in the local cinema, a relic of enemy occupation, these turns being enormously appreciated by all.

During this period officers kept touch with

the march of events in the Corps area, frequently visiting the line for general reconnaissance, and maintaining a general study and interest in the operations.

In the midst of this comparative peace and prosperity came the news of a further need for Whippets.

On November 1, orders were received for the attendance at a conference at the VI. Corps Headquarters, Major J. Leslie, D.S.O., M.C., complying with this order.

<small>Preparations for Battle of Maubeuge-Mons.</small>

Orders were received from the 2nd Tank Brigade on the day following that this Battalion, comprising twelve Whippets, were to operate with the VI. Corps, to be used with the cavalry, as a screen for the infantry from the Brown Line to Maubeuge, on Z plus 1 day.

The Battalion commander and the Company commander visited Corps and Brigades, and personally saw all the commanding officers of the infantry they had to work with. All Company commanders met their C.O. and officers of the infantry with whom they were operating.

Thirteen Whippets formed a Composite Company under Major J. Leslie, D.S.O., M.C., and left Elincourt on November 2. They were ordered to lie up between Haussie and La Capelle. Farm de Rieux was reached at 4 P.M. after completing trek.

The " A " crews had meanwhile been despatched by lorry to Quievy, where they were comfortably billeted. By orders of the VI. Corps the Tanks were to move to a point northeast of La Capelle, on the night of the 3rd, being directly under the orders of the VI. Corps. This 3000 yards took some $7\frac{1}{2}$ hours to accomplish, two rivers had to be crossed, and there were no bridges strong enough for the Tanks. O.C. Company was particularly requested to avoid Escarmain, for fear of impeding the concentration, otherwise he would have made use of the ford in this village.

Three Whippets became ditched in various parts of the rivers, whilst everyone but the first had to be towed out. To give some impression of the state of the stream, no sooner had Tank A. 351 got its tail in the river than the water was up to the driver's waist and into the engine.

Nine Whippets eventually reached the point arranged, north-east of La Capelle, where they parked up for the night. The " A " crews left the billets as soon as the Tanks were parked up, and spent the remainder of the night with the " B " crews, under the Tanks, taking over from the " B " crews at dawn, when a hot meal and tea was brought up to them in food-containers.

Orders from the VI. Corps were to follow the battle at a distance, and get to a position where the Tanks could go in at dawn, on Z plus 1 day, with the 3rd Guards Brigade, or Oxford Hussars,

Following the Battle.

according to the opportunity the situation might afford. As the Blue Line was practically captured before dawn the Tanks moved forward at 8 A.M. to the Halte. O.C. Company kept in touch with the 1st and 2nd Guards Brigades at Mortry Farm to ascertan the progress. Meanwhile the route was reconnoitred over the Rhonelle and subsidiary stream.

At 10 A.M. the infantry were reported to be moving into the Green Line and the Tanks were ordered forward.

One Tank had developed a leaky radiator at the lying-up point, and another broke a fan belt near the Halte. The remaining seven, with the aid of spuds and towing, succeeded in crossing the Rhonelle, and reached a point on the reverse slope of the ridge, where a halt was made. O.C. Company was then in touch with the 1st and 2nd Guards Brigades, whose Headquarters were at Les Quatrevents. The infantry halted for the night about 1000 yards in front of the Green Line, through Wargnies and Bergignies. O.C. Company decided to lie up for the night in Flaque Wood. Tank A. 290 had to be left behind, the big end giving out.

The Company rallying-point was selected at Le Bracmar.

At 6 A.M. on the morning of the 5th, Z plus 1 day, the 3rd Guards Brigade, having pushed through the 1st and 2nd Brigades, were ordered

FROM TINCOURT TO ELINCOURT 193

to continue the advance by bounds. The Red Line was to be taken, then the line east of Preux, the third and fourth objectives being a line north and south through Bermeries and Buvignies respectively.

So far, although VI. Corps were acquainted with all movements of the Tanks, no orders had been received from them. It was obvious from the nature of the country, and the machine-gun opposition on the side of the enemy, that a break through by the Corps' mobile troops was out of the question. The condition of the roads, which prevented our supplies from reaching us by lorry, also the state of the going for the Whippets, had to be taken into consideration. Under the circumstances it appeared that it was a physical impossibility for the Tanks to operate further than the Brown Line, which ran north-west and south-east through Bavay. Since no orders had been received from the VI. Corps, O.C. Company decided to operate with the 3rd Guards Brigade, and endeavour to put them on the Brown Line. This was agreed to by the G.O.C. 3rd Guards Brigade, whose Headquarters was in Flague Wood.

O.C. Company decided that the Tanks could more effectually operate over the second, third and final objectives than over the daylight attack, as it was problematical as to where the Bultiaux River could be crossed.

194 THE SIXTH TANK BATTALION

At 6 A.M. Major Leslie ordered the Tanks to move to a point 1000 yards north-east of Flague Wood, whilst he then reported to the O.C. 2nd Scots Guards, and 3rd Grenadiers. It was decided that the Whippets should endeavour to cross Bultiaux near Le Warpe, and proceed forward with the 2nd Scots Guards until the nature of the ground allowed the Tanks to deploy over the Divisional frontage (*i.e.* two Battalion fronts). Major Leslie rode on to Preux, and ascertained that the Tanks could cross a bridge some 700 yards to the right of Preux, which had not been blown up by the enemy. The Tanks, six in number, were ordered to proceed to Le Bracmar, where a conference was held with the O.C. 2nd Scots Guards, to decide a plan of attack. It was decided that the infantry, who were holding a line through Brettrechies–Le Bracmar, should advance in co-operation with the Whippets and capture Bermeries and Buvignies, and finally the Brown Line.

The attack was to start at 10 A.M. The Whippets were taken to Bout-la-Haut by road.

Action with Guards on November 5. The leading Company of the 2nd Scots Guards was concentrated in a sunken road north of Bout-la-Haut, and was meeting with considerable machine-gun fire when any attempt to advance had been made. O.C. Company then despatched three Tanks under Lieut. C. B. Plant in a north-easterly direction, one going through Bermeries, and the other two round the west of Bermeries, to cover the infantry advance. Two more under Lieut. A. W. Brock were despatched towards the railway, about 400 yards to the right of Farm de Cambren, to cover the advance of the Grenadiers. The nature of the ground was most favourable for the Whippets. It consisted chiefly of orchards, with 20 feet hedges, and ditches, which afforded excellent cover for the enemy machine guns, rendering them extremely difficult to locate.

As soon as the Tanks under Lieut. Brock left the road east of Bout-la-Haut, they drew heavy machine-gun fire. They were instructed to fire short bursts along the hedgerows and railway bank for moral effect, even if no enemy were visible. This they succeeded in doing, and found a few fleeting targets before returning to get into touch with the infantry. Lieut. Brock was slightly wounded in the head by a bullet penetrating the armour plating.

The three Tanks which had proceeded in a north-easterly direction had strict orders not to lose touch with the infantry. Lieut. H. F. Jones, who was on the right of Lieut. Plant, observed a battery firing at Lieut. Plant in a certain neighbourhood north-east of Buvignies. This was dispersed when fired on. Two machine-gun teams were put out of action, and many bursts of fire were put on to hedgerows which might contain enemy. In the meanwhile the O.C. Grenadiers discovered that his right flank was in the air, and he did not consider it prudent to advance. The Scots Guards made their way through Bermeries, without casualties, eventually stopping for the night on a line in the vicinity of Buvignies.

Lieuts. Jones and Plant came back to the Scots Guards in Bermeries, and an attempt was again made to capture and consolidate on the high ground through Buvignies. The driver of Lieut. Plant's Tank was hit, in endeavouring to rectify a minor mechanical trouble, and Lieut. Plant then got on to Lieut. Jones's Tank and proceeded forward. It appears that the Tank in endeavouring to run over the enemy rifle-pits ran on to a tree stump, and stopped behind the enemy's lines in Buvisiaux, where it was afterwards found. The crew, consisting of Lieuts. Jones and Plant, the driver and the gunner, were missing. From accounts of civilians who were then behind the enemy's lines, it appears that they were taken prisoners at midnight, the Tank being blown up. They also reported that after the Tanks had been through Buvignies the enemy hurriedly departed, and also vacated the railway, which had been holding up the Grenadiers. This enabled the

FROM TINCOURT TO ELINCOURT

3rd Guards Brigade to push forward during the night some 2000 yards without opposition. At nightfall the remaining four Whippets were ordered to rally at a point between Le Bracmar and Amfroipret.

It was decided not to use the remaining Whippets on the following day, and work was concentrated on getting fit the six Whippets which might be made available to fight or trek. This was completed on the night of the 7th, when orders were received to trek back to La Capelle.

The distance accomplished by the Tanks in action and back to La Capelle was 54 miles.

In the modern method of attack, *i.e.* without a preliminary bombardment, there are not enough infantry to support Tanks, unless reserve companies are used. Consequently any attack by Tanks must be carefully prepared beforehand, and this practically precludes the possibility of successfully seizing fleeting opportunities to penetrate the enemy's positions deeply, especially as Tanks cannot be relied on to keep free from mechanical trouble.

The following are the casualties for this action : Casualties.

Wounded.
2/Lieut. A. W. Brock.
92523 Private Muirhead, J.
305497 ,, Britton, W.
205613 ,, Forward, I. R.

Prisoners of War.
2/Lieut. C. B. Plant.
„ H. F. Jones.
201205 Private Ross, G.
69722 „ Jeffrey, C. G.

Six Whippets returned to La Capelle, along the old routes, on the morning of the 8th, Major J. Leslie, D.S.O., M.C., riding on in advance, and arranging billets for the Company on arrival.

Move to Quievy.
On November 9, Battalion Headquarters moved from Elincourt to Quievy, a village partially evacuated, and in good condition. Excellent billets were available for the Battalion, the six Tanks and personnel of the Composite Company, under Major Leslie, trekking from Capelle, and rejoining the Battalion at Quievy.

On the 10th the Tanks left at Elincourt on the 2nd, now being repaired and in trekking condition, moved from the Tankodrome at Elincourt, and joined the remaining Tanks of the Battalion already at Quievy.

All stores, details, etc. were lorried to Quievy from Elincourt. This day the rumours of a long-expected Armistice became prevalent, in many circles it being stated that the signing of the Armistice was now a certainty.

Armistice.
On November 11 a wire was received from the 2nd Tank Brigade confirming the signing of the Armistice, and cessation of hostilities at 11 A.M. This news produced the expected effect upon the men, the occasion being celebrated

by a firework display entirely impromptu. A large stock of Bosche Véry lights, and signal rockets, of every imaginable colour and type, being fired indiscriminately in all directions.

From this time onwards sports and amusements were seriously considered, and all possible arrangements made to keep the men interested and fit. Football matches with local R.A.F. teams were arranged, and inter-Company matches drawn up.

Preliminary movement orders were received of a possible move by the Battalion on or about the 18th. Again Madame Rumour held sway, and many were the conjectures as to the possible destination, the extreme views being Germany and the Rhine, and also Wailly.

To relieve the monotony of the daily Tankodrome parade, Colonel Lord Somers instituted a Battalion Whippet race, the course extending about 1 mile, on ground to the east of Quievy. Minor excitements were provided for the spectators by a series of jumps, and a dry-stream crossing. This race proved most successful, drivers having a test of their capabilities, and distance judging, the winner making an easy first, after taking an optional jump of about 15 feet into the dry river-bed, thereby shortening his course.

St. Vaast was advised as being the entrainment point for the move. The route to this

200 THE SIXTH TANK BATTALION

station was examined, and all preparations made for the trekking, a short journey of about two miles only.

<small>Move to Blangy.</small> On the 19th, movement orders and train-table were received for the entrainment on the following day, the destination now being known to be Blingel Camp, in the Tank Corps area. An advanced party was despatched by lorry to take over the camp, and allot accommodation. On arrival at Blingel this party was informed that the Battalion was to be billeted in Blangy-sur-Ternoise. They accordingly took over billets in Blangy, and prepared, as far as possible, for the arrival of the Battalion from Erin.

Two trains were provided at St. Vaast for the Battalion, a few covered trucks also being included of the variety " 40 Hommes 8 Chevaux." The Whippets for the first train trekked to St. Vaast on the 20th, parking up in a field by the railway, under a guard, crews returning to billets, as the train was not due to leave until noon 21st.

On the following day Battalion Headquarters moved from St. Vaast to Blangy, stores, details, etc., proceeding by train.

Tanks entrained successfully at St. Vaast, and left about 10 P.M. This train arrived at Erin in darkness, about 6 P.M. on the 22nd. As the men were comfortable in trucks, and shunting difficult, it was decided to

FROM TINCOURT TO ELINCOURT 201

remain at Erin during the night, and detrain at 7 A.M.

The second train from St. Vaast left at 1 P.M. on the 23rd, arriving at Erin in good time about dawn. All Whippets of both trains were detrained without trouble, and trekked to the Tankodrome at Blangy during the morning.

Billets in Blangy proved to be sadly in need of repair, several days being spent by all available men in executing the necessary repairs to make the billets habitable.

On November 25 a party consisting of one officer and eight men proceeded to Neuvillette to trek the two Tanks left there on September 22. A train had been arranged at Saulty for a supply section of Tanks, and it was decided to trek the two Whippets to Saulty, and entrain there for Erin, in preference to trekking the Whippets to Blangy. The Whippets left Neuvillette on November 25 at 3 P.M. and arrived at Saulty Station on the following morning at 1.30 A.M., without incident. Here, as usual, no news or information could be obtained regarding the train. A Tank train eventually sauntered into the station during the morning of the 28th, the two Whippets entraining about 12 noon. This train arrived at Erin at 5 P.M. on the 29th. Tanks were then detrained, and the two Whippets driven to Blangy and parked up.

Owing to the inadequate accommodation,

Improvements to Camp.

and the need of additional huts for winter training, recreation huts, cinema, etc., fifteen Nissen huts and two standard huts were obtained from the R.E. dump at Erin. These have been erected on a portion of the field used as the Tankodrome.

The usual winter training courses have been commenced, and are now in full swing.

As the courses at Le Tréport had been cancelled, Battalion courses were necessary. Work was continued by all during the mornings, the afternoons being devoted to sports and recreational training.

Brigade competitions were organised under Battalion committees, a keen interest being displayed by the men. Three football grounds were arranged for, and frequent trial and interCompany matches played.

An interesting Ceremonial Parade took place at the 3rd Tank Brigade Headquarters, Estuville Château, on Sunday, December 1; Major-General Sir H. J. Elles, K.C.M.G., C.B., D.S.O., G.O.C. Tank Corps in the Field, presenting N.C.O.'s and men awarded honours or mentions with the special Tank Corps Whistle Cord.

The following honours and awards were granted to the Battalion for the actions referred to in this chapter :

Bar to Military Cross
Lieut. F. F. Bromley, M.C.

Military Cross.
2/Lieut. J. A. H. Holloway.
  ,,   J. C. Hodgens.
Captain C. North.

Distinguished Conduct Medal.
308428 Private Quinn, F.

Bar to Military Medal.
201212 Sergeant Hunter, B., M.M.

Military Medal.
305531 Private Payne, F. G.
 92813   ,,   Cowley, J.
306252 Lance-Corporal Richardson, E. H.
 92991 Corporal Bridges, G.
 69720   ,,   Howlett, G. F.
201236   ,,   Lewis, E.
201813 Private Bishop, C.

201050 SERGT. DUDLEY, T. J., D.C.M.   69647 PTE. BREAKEY, W., D.C.M.
77365 SERGT. PREST, W., D.C.M.
69575 PTE. MORREY, W., D.C.M.   62995 CPL. BUSSEY, B. F., D.C.M.

APPENDIX I

SIXTH TANK BATTALION

Honours and Awards

V.C.	1
Bar to D.S.O.	2
D.S.O.	4
Bar to M.C.	3
M.C.	29
D.C.M.	11
Bar to M.M.	1
M.M.	44
M.S.M.	5
Medaille Militaire	1
Croix de Guerre	1
Belgian Croix de Guerre	2

ROLL OF HONOURS AWARDED SINCE THE LANDING OF THE BATTALION IN FRANCE

V.C.
Lieut.-Colonel R. A. WEST, D.S.O., M.C.

Bar to D.S.O.
Lieut.-Colonel R. A. WEST, V.C., D.S.O., M.C.
Major P. HAMOND, D.S.O., M.C.

D.S.O.
Lieut.-Colonel LORD SOMERS, M.C.
Major C. F. HAWKINS, M.C.
Major J. LESLIE, M.C.
Major A. H. RYCROFT

Bar to M.C.

Major T. K. ROBSON, M.C.
Captain F. F. BROMLEY, M.C.
Captain G. P. VOSS, M.C.

M.C.

Lieut.-Colonel R. A. WEST, V.C., D.S.O.
Major T. K. ROBSON
Captain A. H. C. BORGER
Captain F. F. BROMLEY
Captain A. R. CHAPMAN
Captain D. A. S. F. COLE
Captain E. N. EDWARDS
Captain W. F. FARRAR
Captain W. HORSLEY
Captain J. L. LEES
Captain H. N. MORTON
Captain J. MUNRO
Captain R. M'GILL, R.A.M.C.
Captain C. NORTH
Captain D. H. RICHARDSON
Captain W. E. H. SCUPHAM
Captain J. A. THURSTON
Captain A. L. WATKINS
2/Lieut. H. A. AVINS
2/Lieut. A. W. FLETCHER
2/Lieut. L. C. GROUTAGE
2/Lieut. G. HILL, D.C.M.
Lieut. J. C. HODGENS
2/Lieut. J. A. H. HOLLOWAY
2/Lieut. E. P. IRELAND
Lieut. E. S. LENNARD
2/Lieut. A. E. RENWICK
2/Lieut. C. H. J. TOLLEY
Lieut. C. WATERHOUSE

Croix de Guerre.

Captain G. M. MELLOR

Belgian Croix de Guerre.

Captain D. H. RICHARDSON, M.C.

APPENDIX I

D.C.M.

69715	C.S.M.	CUTHBERT, F. W.
201050	Sergeant	DUDLEY, T. J.
78690	C.S.M.	MISSEN, R. F.
69575	Private	MORREY, W.
69647	,,	BREAKEY, W.
91977	L.-Cpl.	BURDEN, L. J.
92870	Sergeant	BREWER, J. V.
77365	,,	PREST, W.
93000	Private	SIDELL, W.
92995	Corporal	BUSSEY, B. F.
308428	Private	QUINN, F.

Bar to M.M.

201212	Sergeant	HUNTER, B., M.M.

M.M.

95512	Sergeant	HARRINGTON, G. W.
38746	Private	DOWSE, G.
92352	,,	CORBY, J.
38894	,,	FRANCOMBE, C.
92687	,,	YOUNG, B. S.
201060	L.-Cpl.	TARRY, A. J. W.
92565	Sergeant	HORNSEY, C. G.
69726	,,	CALTON, E. J.
69629	Private	HAYTON, E. W.
69463	,,	ARTHURS, F. C.
69751	,,	BUDD, P. E.
69468	,,	BINLEY, J. H.
92716	C.S.M.	ABEL, C.
69619	Sergeant	DOLLEY, T. W.
92354	,,	BARRETT, W.
69540	,,	ARNELL, F.
201078	,,	SILVESTER, G.
201185	Private	ALWAY, A.
201212	Sergeant	HUNTER, B.
69432	L.-Cpl.	PASCOE, A.
201747	Sergeant	TEBBUTT, W.
69415	,,	PHILLIPS, G. W.

92530	Private	MOODIE, R. K.
165295	,,	VOWLES, P. J.
201106	L.-Cpl.	KERR, T. D.
111481	Private	IRELAND, D. M.
92353	,,	RENNIE, J.
201168	,,	MATTOCKS, B. S.
69635	,,	THOMAS, C.
201806	Sergeant	SMETHURST, J.
309077	L.-Cpl.	BALLS, T. H.
69537	Corporal	PETERSON, M.
69638	Sergeant	COSSUM, F. H.
93011	L.-Cpl.	BROWN, F. A.
93009	Corporal	STANNARD, H. V.
305933	,,	SHOOTER, W.
305531	,,	PAYNE, F.
92313	Private	COWLEY, J.
306252	L.-Cpl.	RICHARDSON, E. H.
92991	Sergeant	BRIDGES, G.
69720	,,	HOWLETT, G. F.
201236	Corporal	LEWIS, G.
201813	L.-Cpl.	BISHOP, C.
69654	Corporal	Barker, G. S.

M.S.M.

201017	Corporal	STOKES, W. W.
201034	Private	REID, W. H.
69723	S.-Sergt.	WETHERALL, C.
	R.Q.M.S.	HARRIS
	S.-Sergt.	KENNETT

Medaille Militaire.

92791	Sergeant	WALKER, A.

Belgian Croix de Guerre.

69597	Private	TREW, A. L.

92870 SERGT. BREWER, J. V., D.C.M.   308428 PTE. QUINN, F., D.C.M.
69715 C.S.M. CUTHBERT, F. W., D.C.M.
93000 PTE. SIDDELL, W., D.C.M.   91977 L/CPL. BURDEN, L. J., D.C.M.

APPENDIX II

LIST OF DATES OF ACTIONS FOUGHT BY SIXTH TANK BATTALION

Action.			Date.	No. of Tanks employed.	No. of Tanks rallied.	No. of Casualties.	
						O.	O.R.
Mark IV.							
Ypres	{	Pommern Redoubt	31/1/17	24	8	8	42
		Kansas Cross	22/8/17	8	1	9	38
Cambrai	{	Marcoing	20/11/17	36	29		
		Rumilly	21/11/17	9	9		
		Crêvecœur	21/11/17	4	4	28	139
		Crêvecœur	22/11/17	4	4		
		Bourlon	27/11/17	17	9		
		Fontaine	27/11/17	9	7		
St. Leger			22/3/18	2	2		
Medium Mark " A "							
Villers-Bretonneux			8/8/18	31	25	9	9
Rosières			9/8/18	24	20	7	9
Parvillers			10/8/18	14	7	1	2
Ayette			21/8/18	23	21	5	3
Ervillers			23/8/18	15	8	9	12
Mory Copse			31/8/18	4	4	0	0
Mory Copse			1/9/18	5	5	0	0
Bray			22/8/18	4	4	1	0
Happy Valley			24/8/18	3	2	0	0
Vaulx Vraucourt			1/9/18	2	1	2	3
St. Leger			2/9/18	2	2	0	3
Hermies			3/9/18	6	4	0	0
Lehancourt Ridge			29/9/18	9	8	0	0
Joncourt			30/9/18	3	1	1	1

Action.	Date.	No. of Tanks employed.	No. of Tanks rallied.	No. of Casualties.	
				O.	O.R.
Brancourt	8/10/18	6	3 ⎫	7	14
Premont	8/10/18	17	14 ⎭		
Molain	17/10/18	4	1	1	11
Bout-la-Haut	5/11/18	5	4	3	5
Shelling of Camp at Wailly	21/3/18	..	..	1	14

A total of 27 separate actions, 290 Tanks employed, 207 Tanks rallied, 83 Tanks being knocked out.

Total casualties: 92 officers and 305 other ranks.

MEDIUM MARK "A" TANK.

APPENDIX III

NOMINAL ROLL OF ALL OFFICERS AND MEN WHO HAVE SERVED WITH THE BATTALION IN FRANCE.

No.	Rank.	Name.
69450	Sergeant	Arnell, F.
201143	,,	Appleby, C. P.
92716	R.S.M.	Abel, C.
69480	Private	Adams, W. C.
69425	,,	Allen, W. H.
69538	,,	Anstey, J. T.
69463	,,	Arthurs, F. C.
69510	,,	Ashdown, H. B.
69587	,,	Ayling, J. J.
92986	,,	Alcock, G. W.
95288	,,	Ashmore, W. M.
306844	,,	Abbott, G. W.
306465	,,	Acott, F.
69247	,,	Anderson, G. W.
95785	,,	Adrews, E. F.
302415	,,	Anderson, E. W.
201054	Corporal	Adamson, E. S.
2145	Private	Allen, A. P.
92457	,,	Ashplant, W.
92583	,,	Anderson, H. T.
201185	,,	Alway, A. R.
38893	,,	Atkinson, T.
201167	,,	Attfield, F.
92645	,,	Atkinson, W.
201059	Corporal	Bulmer, E. E.
201173	Sergeant	Buckel, J. F.

No.	Rank.	Name.
69716	Corporal	Barker, W.
201207	Sergeant	Bristoe, J.
201176	Private	Bullevant, G. F.
201219	,,	Bowden, S.
201165	,,	Belton, P. J.
201228	,,	Ballard, A. H.
92692	,,	Belles
201197	,,	Birchdale, R.
92686	,,	Bevant, T.
201092	,,	Bessant, W.
92694	,,	Buckley, C.
201715	,,	Bingham, E. H.
201244	,,	Bloomfield, E.
92667	,,	Brown, J.
306765	,,	Burrell, S. A.
306284	,,	Barnes, G. M. E.
92867	Sergeant	Brewer, J. V.
315512	Private	Bannister, O. S.
315831	,,	Bacons, S.
315651	,,	Barnes, J. T.
315514	,,	Bailey, A.
315517	,,	Bird, J.
316843	,,	Bailey, T. I.
44	Sergeant	Burt, H. L.
308998	,,	Brown, L.
95648	Private	Bird, T. W.
96890	,,	Bailey, W. S.
201813	,,	Bishop, C.
15194	,,	Brennan, W.
69505	,,	Byrne, T.
96788	,,	Boyd, G. W.
307888	L.-Cpl.	Bower, E. C.
307086	Private	Baker, W.
69701	,,	Burton, M. J. W.
201155	Sergeant	Burchett, J. E.
201127	L.-Cpl.	Bithery, L. C.
201182	Corporal	Blowers, W.
2594	,,	Baldock
201119	Private	Bessant, F.

APPENDIX III

No.	Rank.	Name.
201095	Private	Bott, A. R.
201150	,,	Bennett, H. S.
201141	Sergeant	Brereton, T.
201146	Private	Bell, W. H.
69556	,,	Barnett
	,,	Barratt, G. A.
69254	,,	Brown, A.
69540	,,	Barton, M.
69284	,,	Bowers, B. T.
69301	,,	Brown, A. H.
69514	,,	Bews, W. E.
69376	,,	Baker, A. J. W.
201187	,,	Biggerstaff, E. A.
92641	,,	Baker, E.
201244	,,	Bursford, A.
201254	,,	Breeze, S.
201181	,,	Bradford, R.
92511	,,	Butler, L.
69654	,,	Barker, G. S.
69511	Corporal	Bales, E. J.
69615	Private	Barnsby, E. L.
69451	,,	Bragley, C. E.
69559	,,	Biggen, F. J.
69515	,,	Blackwell, C. A.
69648	,,	Binley, J. H.
69456	Corporal	Bond, W.
69447	Private	Bossey, A. C.
69524	,,	Braedy, E.
69492	,,	Bradley, E. C.
69647	,,	Breakey, W.
69227	,,	Broughton, J. A.
69499	,,	Bush, F. W.
69571	,,	Budd, P. E.
92354	,,	Barrett, T. W.
	,,	Bendall, J. A.
69378	,,	Bishop, A.
92584	,,	Brown, J.
92564	,,	Bergman, A. F.
	,,	Barber, W. W.

THE SIXTH TANK BATTALION

No.	Rank.	Name.
92592	Private	Byrne, M.
	,,	Backshale, A.
91759	Sergeant	Bowman, S. G.
69404	Private	Benton, W.
201081	Corporal	Beminster, W. H.
		Brown, F.
92544	Private	Bayne, A.
		Brown, R.
		Broom, H.
92995	Private	Bussey, B. F.
92998	Sergeant	Bridges, G.
93011	Private	Brown, F. A.
93001	,,	Bowers, H. R.
91764	,,	Borrow, T. E.
95767	,,	Bulgar, J. G.
2934	A.S.S.	Barlow, T.
92479	Private	Blakesley, S.
27780	,,	Burton, W.
95467	Corporal	Boxall, W.
92903	Private	Blight, H. G.
203783	,,	Brier, E.
316803	,,	Bulman, B.
69648	,,	Binley, J. H.
112360	,,	Browning, A. J.
303023	,,	Boxale, E. S.
305235	,,	Black, W.
302668	,,	Bilcliffe, G. L.
306261	,,	Brown, J.
306234	,,	Blake, G. B.
306290	,,	Boyd, W.
306580	,,	Beyson, R.
308077	L.-Cpl.	Bale, T. H.
305179	Private	Brittian
95472	Sergeant	Beer, A. L.
91974	Private	Boddy, H.
92838	,,	Brown, J. M.
205323	,,	Bestwick, W. S.
201045	,,	Carter, L.
201049	,,	Clarke, A.

APPENDIX III

No.	Rank.	Name.
69285	Private	Craswell, F. E.
69349	,,	Cordon, B. A.
69396	,,	Chew, A. M.
92454	,,	Connor, A.
92465	,,	Cross, F. H.
92472	,,	Constable, E.
92525	,,	Copeman, E. W.
92526	,,	Cargill, G.
92546	L.-Cpl.	Cumming, D.
92585	Private	Cooke, J. A.
92593	,,	Courtney, F. G.
92599	,,	Canovan, J.
92614	,,	Craggs, F. J.
92476	Sergeant	Clarke, M. K.
201131	C.Q.M.S.	Callaghan, E.
201067	L.-Cpl.	Crossley, B.
92772	Private	Castleman, S.
201149	,,	Cooke, G. G.
69534	,,	Cooper, H.
92533	,,	Campbell, H.
201079	Corporal	Crummie, J.
92822	Private	Cook, S.
201966	,,	Carmie, W. J.
92414	,,	Cobain, W.
11811	,,	Cragg, F. H.
112304	,,	Clarkson, J.
305778	,,	Cross, T. J.
69726	Sergeant	Calton, E. L.
93012	Private	Cushing, H. R.
69638	Corporal	Cossum, H.
69655	,,	Colter, A. L.
69591	L.-Cpl.	Cook, F. H.
69617	Private	Croxton, J.
95317	,,	Campteb, T.
95780	,,	Carter, H. H.
75576	,,	Clark, E.
90886	,,	Crisp, F. N.
103933	,,	Chipperfield, C.
201239	,,	Cox, G. A.

THE SIXTH TANK BATTALION

No.	Rank.	Name.
201193	Corporal	Cox, H.
201215	Private	Chapman
201153	C.Q.M.S.	Cook, W. H.
69715	C.S.M.	Cuthbert, F.
201214	Sergeant	Cox, H. P.
201253	L.-Cpl.	Clayton, T.
201142	Private	Champion, A. J.
201118	,,	Cruson, H. C.
92352	Corporal	Corby, J.
92661	Private	Croucher, G.
92640	,,	Cheshire, F. A.
92671	,,	Coutts, R.
92681	L.-Cpl.	Coglan, H.
92648	Private	Cousins, P.
38913	,,	Cox, J.
69431	,,	Campbell, J.
69616	,,	Chester, F.
69395	,,	Clark, H. C.
69579	,,	Clifford, J. B.
69596	,,	Cockshutt, R.
69523	,,	Cole, C.
69890	,,	Cotterill, E. E.
69236	,,	Collongs, W.
6967	,,	Croxton, J.
69650	,,	Curtis, J.
69651	,,	Curtis, J. K.
92715	,,	Collongs, R.
92488	,,	Casburn, J.
92525	,,	Copeman, E. D.
92847	,,	Connolly, J.
95258	,,	Champion, H.
306907	,,	Collons, G.
110290	,,	Coatley, J.
92313	,,	Cowley, J.
316117	,,	Cox, W.
306160	,,	Collier, A.
201906	,,	Crapper, E.
306230	,,	Cook, S. J.
302525	,,	Cooper, A. C.

APPENDIX III

No.	Rank.	Name.
40381	Sergeant	Cameron
95448	Private	Cook, F. C.
94912	,,	Canterill, F.
179	,,	Crofts, J.
251527	,,	Collingsor, R.
191348	,,	Connelly, T.
11715	,,	Coltas, W.
306514	,,	Clark, H. W.
93005	,,	Collings, R. J.
309083	,,	Cuthbert, J.
306176	,,	Daniels, E. W.
306198	,,	Duthie, J.
94880	,,	Day, F. W.
94970	,,	Drake, A. E. J.
92278	,,	Dunstan, H. A.
111758	,,	Davies, A.
110192	,,	Davies, J. J.
305875	,,	Drew, T. E.
316521	,,	Duggan, W.
316283	,,	Downes, A.
201050	Sergeant	Dudley, T. J.
69709	L.-Cpl.	Dewberry, L. B.
25529	Private	Dransfield, J.
340716	,,	Davies, W. R.
111695	,,	Dibble, E. W.
111433	,,	Dugoir, W.
92323	,,	Donaek, S.
92516	,,	Dalgarno, H.
92625	,,	Day, J. A.
92626	,,	Durden, A. E.
92683	,,	Darwent, A.
69267	,,	Dann, F. G.
69486	,,	Davies, J.
69620	,,	Davies, E. H.
69483	,,	Dennis, E.
69610	,,	Docking, S.
69682	,,	Dodds, G. R.
69619	Sergeant	Dolley, T. W.
69521	Private	Doubleday, C. W.

THE SIXTH TANK BATTALION

No.	Rank.	Name.
69618	Private	Dummer, C. H.
92905	Sergeant	Dolley, W. H.
94809	Private	Denison, A.
92306	,,	Drewery, W.
201866	,,	Davidson, W. T.
92515	Corporal	Davidson, J.
69393	Private	Davis, H.
305815	,,	Deane, S. J.
32451	Sergeant	Davidson, F. R.
69698	,,	Drew
201088	,,	Davies, D. T.
69374	L.-Cpl.	Drewett, W. C.
201124	Private	Dunsmuir, K. M.
69314	,,	Davey, C. C. N.
69536	,,	Dudley, S. R.
92545	,,	Doig, J.
92547	,,	Dalton, P.
92562	,,	Drury, C.
917516	,,	Duyck, L. J.
201075	,,	Dales, A.
78395	,,	Downes, R. N.
201225	,,	Devenish, F.
201125	,,	Dunston, G. C.
201178	,,	Dowse, G.
38829	,,	Dolphin, A. W.
201070	,,	Dimascio, S.
201064	,,	Davies, L. M. J.
201251	,,	Didcote, F.
69689	,,	Dyer, F.
306443	,,	Davies, F.
315108	,,	Dean, C. W.
315121	,,	Davies, J.
316682	,,	Dean, L. E.
201089	,,	Eastham, W. A.
38512	,,	Entwistle, J.
69316	,,	Eagles, A. H.
69894	Sergeant	Ellams, N. H.
92570	Corporal	Ennis, P.
202123	Private	Eyles, T.

APPENDIX III

No.	Rank.	Name
201247	Private	Evrndon, H.
201183	,,	Ellis, C. P.
69563	,,	Edwards, E.
91769	,,	Empson, G. H.
93006	,,	English, A. G.
111473	,,	Ewan, A.
110357	,,	Epps, W. J.
96968	,,	Ealy, F. F.
112760	,,	Edwards, E. P.
111663	,,	Elwood, J. T.
111741	,,	Elcock, E.
111474	,,	Evans, D.
306318	,,	Evans, H. T.
69316	,,	Eagles, A. H.
306348	,,	Edwards, G.
395992	,,	Earl, C.
201123	Sergeant	Fletcher, W. H.
201125	Private	Franks, E.
38514	,,	Flint, P. A.
	,,	Frankland, A.
69224	,,	Foulger, E.
69308	,,	Foster, W. J.
92513	,,	Forrest, W.
	,,	Farmery, T.
92548	,,	Fraser, A.
92613	,,	Fox, E.
	,,	Foster, C. G.
201179	Sergeant	Ford, G.
201147	Private	Forman, J. R.
201208	,,	Franckombe, C.
201103	,,	Frost, C.
69483	,,	Field, S. T.
69512	,,	Fluck, M. W.
69493	,,	Fowler, G.
69684	,,	Francey, A.
69566	,,	Freeth, A. E.
95583	,,	Fox, G. E.
111930	,,	Forrer, F. G.
205210	,,	Francis, H. V.

No.	Rank.	Name.
110244	Private	Foster, J.
306095	,,	Fowler, W.
306000	,,	Fishenden, W. G.
76935	L.-Cpl.	Frost, A. J.
302432	Private	Fraser, F. B.
112609	,,	Frost, H.
111745	,,	Faulkner, G.
111243	,,	Fitton, H.
96588	,,	Fears, H.
307166	,,	Foyle, H. B.
95478	,,	Fenton
205613	,,	Forward, E.
112875	,,	Fraser, G.
96734	,,	Fairley, A. G.
307111	,,	Fraser, J.
305972	,,	Fried, J.
306570	,,	Fielding, H. R.
201112	Sergeant	Greggan, C.
201051	Private	Greener, S.
201121	,,	Garlic, J.
201148	,,	Griffiths, R. N.
201114	,,	Garbutt, R.
69286	,,	Goodchild, J.
925219	,,	Garvie, D.
69712	,,	Gibbs, W.
38708	,,	Gibson
	L.-Cpl.	Girdwood, H.
201221	Corporal	Griffiths
201237	L.-Cpl.	Goodenough
201189	Private	Gilbert, A. E.
201158	,,	Gillitt, E.
201220	,,	Gill, A. E. M.
92776	,,	Green, F.
92621	,,	Gill, H.
92644	,,	Goulstone, N.
92695	,,	Gleave, J. H.
69625	,,	Gilbert, W.
69624	,,	Godfrey, E.
69485	,,	Grey, J.

APPENDIX III

No.	Rank.	Name.
91766	Private	Godley, R.
	,,	Grief, R. J.
201323	,,	Game, H. A.
302507	,,	Graham, J.
201148	,,	Griffiths, R. H.
305815	,,	Gobb, F.
307636	,,	Grimshaw, N.
95359	,,	Gell, W. H.
315700	,,	Gibson, H.
315184	,,	Graham, W. D.
302420	,,	Gibb, J.
201913	,,	Garton, R.
112332	,,	Greenoff, F.
308631	,,	Griggs, P.
306255	,,	Gilbert, C.
315616	,,	Gibson, A.
18817	,,	Graham, T.
241431	,,	Greig, A.
305779	,,	Greentree, W.
98137	,,	Guy, D.
95473	Corporal	Hodges, H. H.
201871	Private	Hancock, P. G.
202873	,,	Hewson, J.
92142	,,	Harding, C.
92876	,,	Hutchings, S. T.
305751	,,	Hutchings, H. L.
307597	,,	Hallom, H. A.
307610	,,	Higgs, A. H. J.
305971	,,	Hislop, J.
306138	,,	Hayes, G.
305843	,,	Humphries, T. J.
301275	,,	Hawkins, S. T.
307063	,,	Harrison, R.
308723	,,	Howe, D.
111701	,,	Hammond, J. J.
316912	,,	Hodson, N.
316620	,,	Hobbs, C. H.
92550	Corporal	Halliburton, A.
	L.-Cpl.	Hooper

No.	Rank.	Name.
	Private	Harrison, W.
95512	Sergeant	Harrington, G. W.
201055	Corporal	Hart, F. A. M.
92620	Private	Halifax, E.
92775	,,	Hopkins
201226	,,	Hatchard
92673	,,	Haddocks, G. S.
201209	,,	Hollingsworth, L.
92628	,,	Hotton, E.
92627	,,	Harding, H.
92643	,,	Hoffman, E. T.
201221	Sergeant	Hutton[1]
201167	L.-Cpl.	Huggett, T.
38736	Private	Hewson, A. W.
69366	,,	Holdsworth, F.
92674	,,	Howat, A. S.
69475	,,	Hinkley, L.
201152	,,	Harlock, A. P.
201212	Sergeant	Hunter, B.
69282	Private	Harris, C. A.
69362	,,	Herbert, S.
69328	,,	Hayes, W. J.
316487	,,	Hardy, A. V.
316251	,,	Howell, B.
315191	,,	Homer, J.
315704	,,	Harris, F.
315900	,,	Holloway, A. E.
315890	,,	Henson, C.
315906	,,	Hourd, A.
315905	,,	Highton, C. A.
315187	,,	Hodson, H. J.
315902	,,	Holroyd, W. C.
315903	,,	Hooper, F.
315203	,,	Harrison, I.
204154	,,	Hursthouse, R.
69516	,,	Harris, V. J.
38910	,,	Hewlitt, S.
92712	Sergeant	Howard, A.
92714	Corporal	Hicks, L. P.

APPENDIX III

No.	Rank.	Name.
92851	Corporal	Howard, A.
69720	,,	Howlitt, G.
40809	Private	Hale, W. T.
201576	,,	Harker, F. G.
205585	,,	Hawkins, S. J.
307023	,,	Hudson, A. V.
316691	,,	Hargraves, W.
316690	,,	Halliwell, J.
315904	,,	Hibberd, H.
315702	,,	Higginbotham, B.
315198	,,	Hanison, W.
31628	,,	Heselden, J.
315705	,,	Hyman, N.
	R.Q.M.S.	Harris, J. M.
92455	Sergeant	Husband
201129	,,	Honeyset, B. G.
201113	L.-Cpl.	Hyman
201115	Private	Hollands, D.
201057	L.-Cpl.	Hill, G.
69573	Sergeant	Hillier, F. C.
69421	Corporal	Holden, W. L.
69249	Private	Harman, G. W.
92463	Corporal	Holden, J.
92477	Private	Horne, G.
92481	,,	Hamer, L.
92565	,,	Hornsey, G.
92590	,,	Hall, C. W. J.
92956	,,	Heffer, J.
69480	,,	Hanna, S.
69442	,,	Hartley, W.
69629	,,	Hayton, E. W.
69652	,,	Herod, W. H.
69645	,,	Harris, W.
69608	,,	Hodgson, E.
69465	,,	Hoy
69561	,,	Houghton, J. H.
69593	,,	Hughes, A. B.
69422	,,	Huntley, R.
92582	,,	Halls, L.

No.	Rank.	Name.
92550	Private	Hallburton, W.
	,,	Howard, G.
302533	,,	Hamer, B.
11645	,,	Hanley, J.
306285	,,	Hill, H. S.
392535	,,	Homer, B.
11724	,,	Hughes, T.
315885	,,	Hanson, H.
201962	,,	Holmes, D.
95737	,,	Howard, G.
97720	,,	Hoddle, A. H.
306607	,,	Hyde, T.
315202	,,	Hardman, W. G.
315884	,,	Hanison, E.
201117	Sergeant	Ingram, H.
201164	,,	Isaac, J. C.
111481	,,	Ireland, B. N.
306204	Private	Irvin, W.
305809	,,	Ireland, W.
316237	,,	Ingall, T. D.
201093	,,	Johns, J. T.
69525	,,	Jinks, W. A.
95510	Sergeant	Jamison, A.
201116	Corporal	Jacobs, W.
69722	Private	Jeffery, C.
69609	,,	Johnston, W. T.
69522	,,	Johnson, F. P.
69494	,,	Jones, S.
93013	,,	Johnson, R. H.
95776	Sergeant	Jenner, G. E.
112572	Private	Jones, R.
306043	,,	Joyce, P.
316913	,,	Johnson, H.
316378	,,	Johnson, C. M.
315288	,,	Joyce, F.
316380	,,	Jenkins, H.
97282	,,	Jeffries, G.
91993	S.-Sergt.	Johnson, J.
316582	Private	Jevons, J.

APPENDIX III

No.	Rank.	Name.
69719	L.-Cpl.	James, W. F.
69668	Private	Joyce, A.
306149	,,	Jackson, W.
306157	,,	Jennings, E.
306484	,,	Jones, D. H.
306543	,,	Jones, E. G.
316855	,,	Jennings, R.
316858	,,	Jenkins, W.
201106	Corporal	Kerr, T. D.
201090	,,	King, J.
201133	Private	Kelsey, F. R.
201137	,,	Kent, A.
69384	,,	Kirk, W.
92699	,,	Kershaw, G.
38618	,,	King, W.
69668	,,	Kerr, E.
69637	,,	Kinsey, G.
69675	,,	Knowles, J.
92997	,,	Kirk, A. A.
93007	,,	Killingback, A.
94887	,,	Kerr, D.
302421	,,	Kearns, W. H.
75760	,,	Kinghton, A. C.
201880	,,	Kirby, F. W.
78620	,,	Kirkham, S.
111393	,,	Keet, H.
316585	,,	Knowles, F.
309102	,,	Kimber, H.
111621	,,	Kirrage, A. E.
201943	,,	Killingly, E.
201082	S.-Sergt.	Kennett, S. E.
305217	Private	Kennedy, J.
301185	Corporal	Lake, R. E.
	Private	Limb, G. H.
302422	,,	Neslie, J. A.
201245	,,	Lyons, A.
201161	,,	Littleproud, N.
69217	,,	Lewis, S. T.
69472	,,	Lewis, N.

No.	Rank.	Name.
92569	Private	Lywood, A. E.
92948	,,	Lowery, H.
69495	,,	Long, J.
91649	,,	Levy, H.
201063	,,	Last, G.
307704	,,	Logan, G. E.
316915	Sergeant	Lancaster, G. E.
316915	Private	Lane, E. J.
69700	Corporal	Lanning, E.
201236	,,	Lewis, E.
201069	L.-Cpl.	Lyle, G.
96436	Private	Lambourne, H.
201109	L.-Cpl.	Latham, P. A.
38410	Private	Leigh, W. H.
201104	,,	Lee, R.
38537	,,	Lee, W. H.
201128	,,	Linsey, A.
201058	Corporal	Laughlan, P.
201125	Sergeant	Langton, L.
92458	Private	Lamb, J. H.
92596	L.-Cpl.	Lewis, J.
201353	Private	Lyle, J.
305836	,,	Lamprey, C. H.
306021	,,	Leatherland, A.
305167	,,	Lennan, T.
316040	,,	Lerrigo, H. W.
302536	,,	Lenn, G.
302544	,,	Law, A.
110257	,,	Lewis, T. O.
77278	,,	Lees, J.
96468	,,	Lewis, A.
306397	,,	Lynas, J.
201052	Sergeant	MacNicoll, A.
92466	,,	M'Avoy, J.
201068	Private	Macdonald, A.
201085	,,	Martin, R.
201097	,,	Mardsen, A.
201100	Sergeant	Molony, J.
201190	,,	Millward, A.

APPENDIX III

No.	Rank.	Name.
201130	Private	Morris, S. J.
92586	,,	Macdonald, D.
93152	,,	Macinroy, R.
92440	,,	Maxwell, A.
69359	,,	Macdonough, A.
95792	,,	Murphy, F.
91861	,,	Mann, J.
302459	,,	M'Lachland, R.
78690	C.S.M.	Missen, R. F.
110367	Private	Moore, J.
306118	,,	MacBride, J. M.
306175	Corporal	Mountfield, J.
96472	Private	Matthews, B. L.
316960	,,	Middleton, G. E.
69752	Corporal	Murphy, V.
69222	Private	Macpherson, J.
70050	Sergeant	Marsh, J. A.
302394	Private	M'Lean, T.
302424	,,	M'Farlane
200183	,,	Mason, R. B.
69221	Corporal	Metcalf, F. E.
69324	Private	Moxey, L. G.
69294	,,	Marshall, J. W.
69368	,,	Mummings, O.
92900	,,	Motherham, F.
92691	,,	Motteram, H.
92629	Corporal	Mathewson, G.
92630	Private	Moody, H.
69583	,,	M'Bride, J.
69478	,,	Martin, W. H.
69448	,,	Matham, G. W.
69543	,,	Maynard, F.
59614	,,	Mee, E. J.
69507	,,	Michael, E. A.
69686	,,	Miller, P.
69409	,,	Mitchell, E. P.
69405	,,	Moss, G.
69575	,,	Morrey, E. W.
92994	,,	Macroe, E.

228 THE SIXTH TANK BATTALION

No.	Rank.	Name.
93014	Private	Marais, F.
69413	,,	Martin, S.
95094	,,	MacCusker, G.
112538	,,	Matthews, G. R.
95473	,,	M'Donnaugh, J.
92900	,,	Motteram, F.
305148	,,	M'Cabe, R. T.
95196	Sergeant	Merredew, P.
305245	Private	M'Rae, J. C.
307624	,,	M'Harrie, R. E.
307681	L.-Cpl.	M'Lennan, A. H.
316406	Private	Mack, A.
316407	,,	M'Guirk, J.
316416	,,	Martland, J. M.
316095	,,	Marr, J.
316219	,,	Mawson, G.
316958	,,	Mackey
92996	L.-Cpl.	Maund, W.
69481	Private	Martin, J.
201812	,,	Marwick, D.
201260	,,	MacNeill, D.
201257	,,	Mortimore, L.
95961	,,	M'Duff, C.
302423	,,	M'Collock, A.
25825	,,	M'Lachlan, R.
111451	,,	M'Kenzie, W.
69424	,,	Mills, F. W.
92523	,,	Muirhead, J.
316268	,,	Malley, P.
201120	Corporal	Merriman, C.
201079	L.-Cpl.	Mead, G.
38492	Private	M'Lennan
201111	,,	Mackie, R.
92460	,,	Mianprize, G.
92551	,,	Mitchell, J.
92597	,,	Measday, S.
91758	L.-Cpl.	Miller, J.
	R.S.M.	Macer, A. H.
		M'Intosh, W.

APPENDIX III

No.	Rank.	Name.
38920	Private	Manzies, R.
92554	,,	M'Norton, S.
201259	Sergeant	Nutter, C.
201053	,,	Murrey, J.
201278	Private	M'Blain, W.
201170	,,	Miller, W.
201188	Corporal	Matthews, D.
201206	Private	M'Rae
201146	,,	Myerss
201166	,,	Mattocks, B.
211171	,,	M'Lennan, A.
201195	,,	Mostyn, H.
92552	Corporal	Newey, L.
69627	,,	Neath, H. J.
92484	Private	Norgate, G. H.
92538	,,	Nicoll, G. H.
92539	,,	Nightingale, L.
201198	,,	Nash, R.
69632	,,	Newberry, E.
92666	,,	Nutter, A.
69409	,,	Newton, H. J.
69364	,,	Newman, E. J.
69678	,,	Nixon, F.
93008	,,	Noble, F. B.
92271	,,	Norman, L.
39467	,,	Nugent, J.
98737	,,	Noward, G.
306400	Corporal	Nevis, C. E.
111665	Private	Nelson, C. H.
69646	L.-Cpl.	Noble, S. A.
69646	,,	Nicholson, C.
306389	Private	Newham, E. J.
308975	,,	Neale, A. C.
308815	,,	Nolan, E.
201204	,,	O'Byrne, C.
69402	,,	Orme, H.
92687	,,	O'Donnell, J.
69508	Corporal	Ould, W.
69280	Private	Olley, A. A.

No.	Rank.	Name.
78688	R.S.M.	O'Keefe, P.
7674	Private	O'Reilly, G.
69432	,,	Pascoe, A.
69640	,,	Peck, C.
69601	,,	Percival, J.
69537	,,	Peterson, M.
69415	,,	Phillips, G.
69502	,,	Philpitt, W.
69445	,,	Polkinghome, W.
69665	,,	Pounder, W.
69533	,,	Prisley, T. R.
95291	,,	Parry, O.
201102	,,	Poole, W.
200313	,,	Peckham, W.
111401	,,	Powell, F.
306025	,,	Phillips, W.
305531	Corporal	Payne, F. G.
316961	Private	Potter, P.
201145	Sergeant	Petts, A. E.
26173	Trooper	Penney, W. J.
309107	Private	Pamphalon, J.
69336	C.Q.M.S.	Patterson, C.
69717	L.-Cpl.	Potter, A. M.
77365	Private	Prest, W.
302508	,,	Penney, E. A.
11653	,,	Pugh, J.
306329	,,	Page, C. C.
305945	,,	Parish, W.
315337	,,	Potter, J. T.
315333	,,	Poskit, R. C.
201102	L.-Cpl.	Poole, W. E.
2691	,,	Parkinson, A.
201108	Private	Payne, F. T.
92483	,,	Pettifer, W.
92528	,,	Penman, T.
92578	,,	Pain, C. F.
92575	,,	Pearson, S. J.
92591	,,	Pleasance, J.
38943	Sergeant	Pasmore, W. L.

APPENDIX III

No.	Rank.	Name.
78691	Sergeant	Pickup, R.
38884	L.-Cpl.	Pick, G.
201247	Corporal	Parkyn, M. J.
201143	Private	Preston, J.
201255	,,	Purser, J.
69295	Sergeant	Payne, A. W.
69268	Private	Potten, E. T.
69357	,,	Price, E. W.
69368	,,	Power, R. L.
92514	,,	Patterson, D.
92646	,,	Pegrum, J. S.
69661	,,	Parnaby, J. J.
69476	Sergeant	Parsons, L.
695200	Private	Quinn, S. W.
308429	,,	Quinn, F.
65464	,,	Richardson, G.
92765	,,	Roberts, T.
94818	,,	Rennolds, H. W.
109692	,,	Redpath, A.
306252	Corporal	Richardson, E.
95795	Private	Robertson, F.
201084	Sergeant	Ritchie, W.
201191	Corporal	Rickard, A. E.
69277	Private	Rook, W.
302381	,,	Rox, D.
109964	,,	Reith, W. J.
69422	,,	Robertson, K. D.
6440	,,	Reed, J.
92353	,,	Rennie, J.
92632	,,	Roberts, C. A.
92638	,,	Read, C. S.
92693	Corporal	Roe, R. C.
201177	Private	Ruffle, W. H.
69513	,,	Reed, G. H.
69519	,,	Reeves, B. G.
69602	,,	Richardson, A.
69504	,,	Roberts, C.
69599	,,	Roy, W.
69676	,,	Rutler, W.

No.	Rank.	Name.
	Private	Rooney, J.
110209	,,	Rogers, E. L.
308721	Corporal	Rogers, J. E.
21973	Private	Rise, A. A.
315366	,,	Ruff, J. F.
69551	Corporal	Richard, H. R.
201046	Private	Riley, A. H.
29677	,,	Richardson, W.
78448	,,	Reeves, A.
201132	Sergeant	Richardson, T.
201092	Private	Rose, A. E.
201134	Sergeant	Read, W. A. L.
201132	,,	Richardson, T.
201092	Private	Rose, B. E.
201134	Sergeant	Read, W. H. L.
38497	Private	Ross, S. J.
92486	Sergeant	Rees, W.
92595	,,	Royston, G. B.
92571	Private	Relf, E.
92522	,,	Ritchie, D. S.
201201	,,	Ruscoe, N.
201205	,,	Ross, G.
201184	,,	Rothweb
201240	,,	Russell, T.
201169	,,	Reeve, C. V.
201244	,,	Robertson, E. C.
201156	,,	Ridgway, H.
201241	,,	Read, A. H.
201157	Corporal	Russon, G. H.
201233	Private	Ribbans, C.
201242	,,	Roberts, R. D.
69381	,,	Rosinck, V.
201073	,,	Starkey, J. B.
201232	,,	San, T.
78684	,,	Scothern, B.
315	,,	Smith, R.
238048	,,	Smith, F.
302425	,,	Stark, J. R.
302309	,,	Shaw, C.
201795	,,	Sedgwick, E.

APPENDIX III

No.	Rank.	Name.
92657	Private	Stephens, D. J.
306119	,,	Sherlock, W. A.
305932	,,	Smith, A. G.
92563	,,	Smith, R.
315892	,,	Shipley, J.
316178	,,	Stevenson, H.
317034	,,	Stradlan, F. J.
92713	Sergeant	Sutton, F.
201077	,,	Stokes, H.
21110	Private	Smale, H.
69228	,,	Sellers, A.
92633	Sergeant	Sanderson, F. W.
92634	Corporal	Stone, H. S.*
92677	Private	Swain, G.
92682	L.-Cpl.	Stevenson, N.
92697	Private	Swindells, W.
		Smith, W. J.
93010	,,	Spirling, T. R.
93016	,,	Steward, W. L.
93009	,,	Stannard, H. V.
69577	,,	Salt, J. K.
69656	,,	Sarson, C. H.
69695	Corporal	Scutt, W. H.
69659	Private	Slater, J. K.
69660	,,	Smith, S.
69530	,,	Smith, B. H.
69528	,,	Spearing, W. T.
92350	,,	Skeerles, T. G.
92999	Corporal	Shred, C. J.
93000	Private	Sidell, W.
93002	,,	Self, A.
69223	Corporal	Simmonds, G. L.
95564	L.-Cpl.	Smith, H.
201313	Private	Skelthon, H.
92866	,,	Southall, B.
201951	,,	Scott, H. W.
111412	,,	Snow, T.
77265	,,	Smith, J. H.
306289	,,	Stunger, A.

* Killed in action.

No.	Rank.	Name.
111590	Private	Sutcliff, G.
302993	,,	Smith, F. A.
318976	,,	Skipp, G. F.
315381	,,	Spooner, W.
316793	,,	Silcock, H.
315814	,,	Smith, J.
315383	,,	Suddick, R.
69660	,,	Smith, S.
201246	,,	Smith, W. J.
201047	Sergeant	Skeldon, A. E.
201098	,,	Silvester, G.*
201122	Private	Swaibrick, J.
92461	,,	Sloan, G.
92459	Corporal	Sayers, A. R.
92485		Sutton, E.
92540	Corporal	Scott, L.
92541	,,	Simpson, J.
		Stein, J.
92563	Private	Smith, R.
92566	,,	Saunders, G.
92586	,,	Southern, W. J.
92598	Corporal	Shears, C. W.
69879	Private	Statby
201158	Sergeant	Siddon, R. E.
201235	L.-Cpl.	Smith, T.
201190	Private	Schrieber, D. W.
201210	,,	Schofield, A.
201203	Sergeant	Such, H.
201186	Private	Smith, W. R.
201168	Sergeant	Smith, P.
201227	Private	Shakespeare, A.†
497	L.-Cpl.	Smith, W. E.
69323	Private	Snelling, J. C.
201094	,,	Starman, A. T.
68877	Sergeant	Smethurst, J.
92097	Private	Sullivan, A.
302510	,,	Sutcliff, T.
8710	,,	Smith, J.
69705	Corporal	Salmon, W. P.

* Military Medal.   † Killed in action.

APPENDIX III

No.	Rank.	Name.
305933	Corporal	Shooter, W. H.
305943	Private	Smith, W.
91413	,,	Swanson, T.
94946	,,	Stokes, A. C.
	Sergeant	Taylor, D. J.
201139	Private	Tucker, E. G.
92449	,,	Tunnicliff, C.*
2256	Corporal	Tarry, A. J. W.
92483	Private	Thatcher, C. W.
A/2924	Arm.-Sergt.	Taylor, L.
201202	Private	Tyson, E.
201238	,,	Tyson, A. N.
69297	,,	Tetley, A. G.
69291	,,	Taylor, S. W.
92635	,,	Try, A. E.
92626	,,	Tucker, A. G.
69611	,,	Taylor, A.
69562	,,	Taylor, J.
69464	,,	Taylor, A.
69497	,,	Taylor, J.
69565	,,	Teague, S.
69603	,,	Thompson, A.
69635	,,	Thomas, C.
69426	,,	Thorne, J. A.
		Thompson, C.
69643	,,	Timson, J. C.
69597	,,	Trew, A.
		Tyler, J.
94829	Corporal	Thorpe, N. E.
201405	Private	Thomson, A. J.
201439	,,	Thornhill, G. H.
92475	,,	Timms, G.
302537	,,	Timmins
200669	,,	Toombes, V.
305982	,,	Tusby, A.
315990	,,	Tucker, A. P.
92678	,,	Thewliss, A.
94889	,,	Tweedie, J. A.
30253	,,	Townsend, F.

* Killed in action.

No.	Rank.	Name.
111732	Private	Thomas, E.
111683	,,	Turnbull, A. E.
305987	,,	Trenby, A. R. J.
78525	,,	Thompson, A.
69380	,,	Thompson, C.
184	,,	Tebbat, W.
95650	,,	Tullock, J. E.
307601	,,	Taccin, W. G.
	,,	Veysey
306256	,,	Vose, G.
201048	Sergeant	Weyham
92452	Corporal	Wallace, W.
201065	Sergeant	Wyatt, T.
201037	Private	Whittaker, P.
201126	,,	Wilson, R. L.
201096	Corporal	White, F. C.
201135	L.-Cpl.	Warren, F.
201183	Private	Wright, E.
201091	,,	Wells, A. R.
7904	,,	Wilson, J.
201061	,,	Warrender, A. B.
69576	,,	Warren, A. H.
		Whitley, H.
92517	,,	Watson, G. B.
92527	,,	Wyatt, B.
92589	,,	Wells, C. W.
92600	,,	Walsh, W. F.
		Whale, N.
201223	,,	Wesley, J.
201200	,,	Wood, C. S.
201180	Sergeant	Williams, E. G.
201076	Private	Woodfield, H. R.
201222	Corporal	Wilson, R.
201249	Private	Willis, B. V.*
92512	Corporal	Watson, J.
69582	Private	Watt, R.
09672	,,	White, T.
69433	,,	Whitemore, G.

* Killed in action.

APPENDIX III

No.	Rank.	Name.
69477	Private	Wild, G. F.
69428	,,	Williams, N. G.
69687	,,	Wilson, T.
69479		Wolfe, A. L.
69429		Wright, H. O.
201048	Sergeant	Weyland, W.
69723	,,	Weatherall, C.
111605	,,	Wood, H.
77311	L.-Cpl.	Wilkins, E.
306381	Private	Wright, T.
307423	,,	Whitby, W.
306491	,,	Werton, W.
306023	,,	Woods, B. G.
317100	,,	Williams, D. J.
316609	,,	Woodcock, L. G.
315468		Whyte, C. C.
201196	L.-Cpl.	Watters, W. H.
201211	Corporal	Wilkinson, W. R.*
110385	,,	Webb, C. J.
78683	Private	White, R. A.
201072	,,	Whiting, J.
306609	Sergeant	Webster, J. A.
112395	Private	Williams, T.
305907	,,	Walker, E. C.
306120	,,	Wilson, A. G.
305822	,,	White, A. W.
305911	,,	Woodhouse, H. E.
92791	,,	Walker, A.
315966	,,	White, M. W.
201248	,,	Yeoman, T.
92637	Corporal	Young, S.
92642	Private	Youard, W.
69427	,,	Young, W.
69438	,,	Yeo, W. H.
92696	,,	Yaffe, S. W.
201194	,,	Young, E. J.
93068	,,	Yates, W.

* Killed in action.

WORKSHOP COMPANY

No.	Rank.	Name.
92127	C.S.M.	Walsgrove, L.
92123	C.Q.M.S.	Burrows, A. S.
38702	Sergeant	Chappel, S. T.
2545	,,	Collier, C.
92136	,,	Galbraith, A. M.
92126	,,	Cronie, P. J.
68771	,,	Warwick, O.
92152	Corporal	Baggaby, S.
92133	,,	Paterson, W.
91984	,,	Ford, S.
91993	,,	Johnstone, J. K.
91978	L.-Cpl.	Bowie, A. S.
38462	,,	Balderson, W. E.
91977	,,	Burden, L. J.
92144	,,	Clarke, C. A.
69699	,,	Fuller, J. E.
91994	,,	Kemp, J. L.
92150	,,	Spratt, W. H.
69721	,,	Payne, C.
91607	,,	Rigden, F. M.
91904	Private	Andrews, H. H.
92942	,,	Armstrong, T.
93141	,,	Armstrong, P.
69247	,,	Anderson, G. W.
69500	,,	Adamthwaite, J. W.
92151	,,	Baker, H. J.
92124	,,	Bull, G.
91995	,,	Ball, H. P.
78396	,,	Bunghay, W.
91987	,,	Burby, W. H.
91975	,,	Bradburn, R. W.
93038	,,	Bale, J. T.
91988	,,	Branagh, H. S.
91986	,,	Brown, G.
91976	,,	Breare, J.
69657	,,	Burden, W. G.

APPENDIX III

No.	Rank.	Name.
69398	Private	Breston, T.
91981	,,	Capewell, C.
91980	,,	Chadwick, C. F.
92001	,,	Clarke, W.
92145	,,	Cooper, P. H.
91982	,,	Chick, A. V.
91996	,,	Croft, R. F.
91990	,,	Cockerhill, F. R.
91979	,,	Clarke, C. J.
91989	,,	Champion, A. G.
69443	,,	Carp, A.
42366	,,	Clubb, R.
91905	,,	Davies, J. R.
91983	,,	Dixon, M. A. E.
91726	,,	Dickens, G.
91997	,,	Fox, F. S.
92584	,,	Freeman, W.
69539	,,	Fanon, C. R.
91999	,,	Glynn, D.
78382	,,	Grey, A. H.
91985	,,	Graziani, L.
92131	,,	Griffiths, H. W.
38865	,,	Godridge, H. J.
91992	,,	Goodale, S.
92278	,,	Dunstan, H.
92138	,,	Hall, G. W.
92000	,,	Hazlehurst, W. E.
91998	,,	Haynes, L. A.
69631	,,	Hart, G.
91772	,,	Hand, F. J.
92142	,,	Harding, C.
69677	,,	Hadway, J.
69373	,,	Hicks, J. A.
91991	,,	Kosh, S. E.
69670	,,	Jones, P. D.
91771	,,	Lodge, H.
92132	,,	Lawrence, H.
92137	,,	Lockyer, W. G.
38549	,,	Hill, W. H.

No.	Rank.	Name.
91912	Private	Meggison, A. W.
91911	,,	Meggison, E. T.
69360	,,	Morris, R.
69222	,,	M'Pherson, J. W.
92711	,,	Myhill, M.
69363	,,	Noke, J. W.
93197	,,	Ormondroyde, A.
68702	,,	Pennock, R. H.
92899	,,	Porter, T.
69391	,,	Pople, W. C.
93193	,,	Padgett, J.
93129	,,	Pearson, J. W.
92774	,,	Pursby, F.
38480	,,	Rimel, C. F.
93153	,,	Rosser, C.
92128	,,	Shaughnessy, P.
92140	,,	Simpson, G.
92797	,,	Shorter, W.
92577	,,	Stripleg, A. D.
91777	,,	Smith, C. A.
69605	,,	Shuttleworth, J.
92474	,,	Spink, A. G.
92773	,,	Stubbings, G.
69444	,,	Strick, S.
92139	,,	Turner, A. O.
92639	,,	Turmaine, A.
78390	,,	Trinder, W.
69393	,,	Snelling, C.
92185	,,	Wiseman, M. H.
92652	,,	Wylde, J. H.
78889	,,	Walters, E. J.
95239	,,	Taylor, A. R.
91813	,,	Lloyd, A. J.
91903	,,	Akehurst, W. H.
2889	,,	Tomkins, S.
2670	,,	M'Adam, L. H.
94917	,,	Borner, J.
92548	,,	Wight, A.

APPENDIX III

OFFICERS

Rank.	Name.
Captain	H. Atherton.
,,	J. Allen, M.C.
Lieutenant	F. Anderson, D.C.M.
,,	C. B. Arnold, D.S.O.
2/Lieut.	E. Avins.
,,	H. K. Ashcroft.
Captain	A. E. Arnold.
,,	W. Arnold.
,,	H. A. Aldridge.
2/Lieut.	S. G. Avery.
,,	J. Black.
,,	G. H. Brooks.
Captain	H. Bown, M.C.
Lieutenant	L. C. Bond, M.C.
2/Lieut.	J. A. Bailey.
,,	A. T. Barton.
,,	N. O. Bennett.
Captain	A. H. C. Borger, M.C.
Lieutenant	A. W. Brock.
2/Lieut.	G. E. Brittain.
,,	H. N. Bates.
Lieutenant	J. C. Butement.
Captain	Bliss (R.A.S.C., attached).
2/Lieut.	N. V. Boulton.
Captain	F. F. Bromley, M.C.
,,	C. E. Curtis.
2/Lieut.	C. W. Carles.
,,	E. Coleman.
,,	A. V. Close.
Captain	W. N. Craigs.
2/Lieut.	R. W. Cartlidge.
,,	W. H. Coley.
,,	J. E. Clarke.
Captain	W. G. Crump.
,,	V. J. Chadd.
2/Lieut.	H. D. Curry.

THE SIXTH TANK BATTALION

Rank.	Name.
Captain	A. R. Chapman, M.C.
,,	E. F. Cunningham.
,,	A. E. Carr.
2/Lieut.	H. E. Colcutt.
Captain	J. A. Crocker.
,,	D. A. S. F. Cole, M.C.
2/Lieut.	I. V. Cummings.
,,	R. A. Dolton.
Major	H. Darby, M.C.
Captain	Sir J. L. Dashwood, Bt.
Lieutenant	S. Doward.
2/Lieut.	R. Davis.
,,	W. A. Duke.
Lieutenant	V. Dupree.
2/Lieut.	G. W. Emery.
,,	F. G. Eckley.
Lieutenant	D. B. Evans.
2/Lieut.	H. A. Enoch.
Captain	E. N. Edwards, M.C.
,,	W. F. Farrar, M.C.
2/Lieut.	R. P. Forster.
,,	A. W. Fletcher.
,,	B. Fife.
Captain	Francis (Chaplain).
2/Lieut.	J. R. Gray.
,,	W. S. Grey.
,,	A. T. C. Gormley.
,,	L. C. Groutage, M.C.
Captain	A. J. Gurr.
2/Lieut.	R. E. Groombridge.
Major	W. O. Gibbs.
Lieutenant	F. R. V. Graham.
Captain	E. J. Hobbs, M.C.
,,	R. E. Howell.
,,	W. Horsley, M.C.
Major	C. F. Hawkins, D.S.O., M.C.
2/Lieut.	R. S. Hay.
,,	W. D. Howell.
Major	P. Hammond, D.S.O., M.C.

APPENDIX III

Rank.	Name.
2/Lieut.	G. Hill.
,,	F. C. Harding
Captain	C. H. Hodge.
2/Lieut.	F. Harris.
,,	N. L. Handford.
,,	C. Handford.
Major	The Hon. P. Henderson.
Lieutenant	C. J. Hodgens, M.C.
2/Lieut.	E. S. Howard.
,,	W. G. Haigs.
,,	J. A. Holloway.
,,	G. B. Heppell.
Major	W. S. Hopkins, M.C.
2/Lieut.	J. A. H. Harries.
,,	J. G. Henderson.
,,	F. H. Harrop.
,,	F. Heald.
,,	C. S. J. Hodges.
Lieutenant	A. Hinxman.
2/Lieut.	S. W. R. Harris.
Captain	H. P. Holt.
Major	A. McC. Inglis, D.S.O.
2/Lieut.	E. P. Ireland, M.C.
,,	E. S. Ingram.
,,	R. F. Innes.
Lieutenant	R. C. Jobling.
2/Lieut.	E. R. Jones.
,,	H. F. Jones.
,,	E. P. Jones.
Lieutenant	E. M. King.
2/Lieut.	H. C. Keating.
Captain	A. G. Kenchington, M.C.
Lieutenant	J. F. Kinneburgh.
Captain	T. A. Kyner (U.S.M.C., attached).
2/Lieut.	E. S. Lennard.
Captain	W. H. G. Laycock.
2/Lieut.	W. de B. Leach.
,,	D. V. Law.
Captain	F. S. Lasky, M.C.

Rank.	Name.
Captain	J. R. Lees, M.C.
Major	J. Leslie, D.S.O., M.C.
2/Lieut.	G. L. Lloyd.
Major	H. Lane, M.C.
Captain	H. W. Mortimore.
Lieutenant	A. P. Macmeeken.
Captain	G. W. Mann.
,,	H. N. Moreton, M.C.
Lieutenant	A. G. Muir.
2/Lieut.	H. A. Mellor.
,,	C. S. Macpherson.
Lieutenant	C. Molyneux.
,,	R. T. Meredith.
2/Lieut.	C. G. W. Moate.
,,	G. Morrell.
,,	W. J. Murray.
,,	A. MacDowell.
Captain	R. MacG. Millar, M.C.
2/Lieut.	A. MacAllister.
,,	J. C. Moston.
Captain	J. Munro, M.C.
2/Lieut.	J. Moss.
Captain	G. M. Mellor.
,,	E. A. W. Maude.
Lieutenant	W. Maughan.
,,	S. C. Mottram.
Captain	R. MacGill (R.A.M.C., attached).
2/Lieut.	W. Millar.
,,	F. F. Moseley.
,,	F. C. Naish.
,,	T. H. Newman.
Captain	F. Neil.
,,	C. North, M.C.
2/Lieut.	N. T. O'Connell.
Captain	J. M. Oke.
2/Lieut.	F. Ogle.
Captain	C. Okell, M.C.
Lieutenant	T. R. Parry (R.A.S.C., attached).
2/Lieut.	H. Pearson, D.C.M.

APPENDIX III

Rank.	Name.
2/Lieut.	A. W. Peters.
,,	G. W. Phillips.
,,	W. A. Paton.
,,	R. G. Purvis.
,,	S. B. Patrick.
Lieutenant	C. B. Plant.
2/Lieut.	W. H. Pollitt.
Captain	A. M. W. Pearson.
2/Lieut.	A. W. Perry.
,,	J. C. Porter.
,,	H. H. Parnell.
Major	G. H. Ross (R.A.M.C., attached).
Captain	A. E. Renwick.
2/Lieut.	R. B. Roach.
,,	A. Ryrie.
,,	N. H. A. Ready.
,,	E. S. Richards.
,,	J. E. Roberts.
Captain	J. A. Renwick.
2/Lieut.	S. C. G. Rich.
Captain	W. Robinow.
2/Lieut.	G. Reed.
Major	T. K. Robson, M.C.
,,	A. H. Rycroft, D.S.O.
Captain	F. S. Roberts.
,,	D. H. Richardson, M.C.
2/Lieut.	A. G. Richardson.
,,	A. S. Robertson.
Lieut.-Colonel	F. Summers, D.S.O., D.S.C.
2/Lieut.	R. Soutar.
,,	A. E. Smith.
Captain	V. G. Sanders.
2/Lieut.	B. Seymour.
,,	F. Sheard.
Captain	W. Start.
,,	A. E. Start.
2/Lieut.	L. Sutherland.
,,	F. Sutton.
Captain	C. Strachan.

Rank.	Name.
Lieutenant	D. N. Shaw.
2/Lieut.	J. L. Simpson.
,,	G. S. Smith.
,,	J. H. Stodel.
Captain	W. L. Stack.
,,	H. S. Sayer.
,,	N. W. Sayer.
2/Lieut.	G. A. Smith.
,,	F. E. S. Sheard.
,,	D. Sutherland.
,,	O. H. Shelswell.
Captain	C. Storey, D.S.O.
,,	W. E. H. Scupham, M.C.
2/Lieut.	V. J. Scottorn.
,,	J. Streeter.
,,	D. M. F. Sheryer.
,,	H. A. Strangman.
,,	G. E. Smith.
,,	K. B. S. Smith.
,,	F. J. Samuels.
Captain	G. A. Shiels (R.A.M.C., attached).
,,	W. Stones, M.C.
2/Lieut.	E. C. M. Shepherd.
Lieut.-Colonel	Lord Somers, D.S.O., M.C.
Lieutenant	E. C. Smithers.
2/Lieut.	H. Seddon.
,,	C. G. H. Tolley, M.C.
Captain	J. A. Thurstan, M.C.
Lieutenant	T. G. L. Taylor.
,,	R. R. Turner.
2/Lieut.	C. E. G. Turner.
Lieut.-Colonel	C. M. Truman, D.S.O.
Captain	J. F. Thompson.
Lieutenant	W. Underhill.
Captain	G. P. Voss, M.C.
2/Lieut.	R. G. Wheatley.
,,	J. Walker.
,,	A. P. Watt.
Lieutenant	A. S. W. Willis.

APPENDIX III

Rank.	Name.
Captain	A. L. Watkins, M.C.
2/Lieut.	J. H. Wylie.
,,	V. S. Wadham.
,,	E. R. Ward.
,,	E. H. Wood.
Lieutenant	C. Waterhouse, M.C.
2/Lieut.	R. J. Whaley.
,,	J. P. Wetenhall.
Lieut.-Colonel	R. B. Wood.
,,	R. A. West, V.C., D.S.O., M.C.
2/Lieut.	A. Wright.

www.ingramcontent.com/pod-product-compliance
Lightning Source LLC
Chambersburg PA
CBHW031137160426
43193CB00008B/173